AN ORIGINAL UNDE

TH

SUMERIAN LEGACY
A GUIDE TO ESOTERIC ARCHAEOLOGY

by
Joshua Free

*Revised, Updated & Expanded 2019 Edition.
Originally published in two installments by the
Mardukite Research Organization in 2010.*

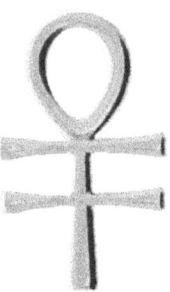

PUBLISHED BY THE **JOSHUA FREE** IMPRINT REPRESENTING
Mardukite Truth Seeker Press — **mardukite.com**

© 2010–2019, JOSHUA FREE

ISBN : 978-0-578-43397-4

No part of this publication may be reproduced in any form or by any means, electronic or mechanical, including photocopying, recording, or by any information storage or retrieval system, without permission in writing from the publisher.

Also available in the hardcover anthology
"Gates of the Necronomicon" by Joshua Free

Cover Graphics by Kyra Kaos

— THE SUMERIAN LEGACY —

Long-lost secrets of ancient Mesopotamian religion, Anunnaki mythology and mysteries of Babylonian magic are coherently revealed in the first complete esoteric guide to Sumerian archaeology accessible to all readers. From the world renown "Mardukite Research Organization" developed by Joshua Free.

This amazing guide to esoteric archaeology reveals the secret Anunnaki tradition of Babylon, forbidden knowledge lost thousands of years.ago— from the origins of Sumerian civilization in ancient Mesopotamia to the rise of Babylonian magic, mythology and religion.

World renown expert and Director of the modern "Mardukite Research Organization" invites the Seeker on an incredible progressive journey to illuminate the most ancient and inaccessible facets of human history, spirituality and religious tradition on the planet.

For the first time ever, anyone can discover the secrets of the Sumerian Anunnaki and the origins of all physical and metaphysical systems born from the Mesopotamian Mystery Tradition that directly led to Babylonian religion— a unique combination of Sumerian, Akkadian, Assyrian and Chaldean lore revealed with perfect clarity for all modern readers: the academic, esoteric and even the "just curious."

Originally published in two installments, this new commemorative edition of *The Sumerian Legacy* collects some of the most critical contributions from the modern "Mardukite Research Organization."

MARDUKITE
10TH ANNIVERSARY

THE
SUMERIAN LEGACY
A GUIDE TO ESOTERIC ARCHAEOLOGY

by
Joshua Free

— TABLET OF CONTENTS —
THE SUMERIAN LEGACY : SECRETS OF THE ANUNNAKI

PART ONE—ANCIENT MESOPOTAMIA
(LIBER 51/52)

0—Esoteric Assyriology of the 21st Century ... 13

1—Mesopotamian Mysteries:
Before Babylon—Land of Sumer ... 17

2—Sargon & The Sumerians:
Divine Right in the Land of Sumer ... 21

3—Sifting Sumerian Sands:
Unearthing the Anunnaki Legacy of Kings ... 25

4—Codes of Hammurabi:
Building Babylon and Beyond ... 29

5—The Kassite Dynasty:
Preserving a Legacy of Legends ... 32

6—Rise of the Assyrians:
From Ashurbanipal to Nebuchadnezzar II ... 34

7—Cuneiform Tablets:
The Birth of World Systems ... 39

8—Priest-Scribes of Nabu:
The Secret Society of Babylon ... 44

9—Mardukite Monolatry:
The Star-Religion of Babylon & Egypt ... 49

10—Marduk & The Anunnaki:
Mesopotamian Mythology in Babylon ... 52

11—Babylonian Magic:
The Art of Priests, Magicians & Kings ... 58

12—Stargates of Babylon:
   The Anunnaki Power of Starfire … 61

13—Mardukite Magic:
   Ancient Rites & Rituals of Eridu … 66

14—"On Earth, Life"
   Akitu : The Babylonian New Year … 70

Epilogue—A Brave New Babylon Rising … 73
   (by "Sortilèges" David Zibert)

PART TWO—THE SUMERIAN ANUNNAKI
(LIBER 50)

00—Abzu: The Primordial Abyss … 79

0—Tiamat: The Primeval Dragon … 84

I—Anu: Kingship in Heaven … 90

II—Enlil: Demiurge of Creation … 96

III—Enki: Lord of this World … 101

   1—Nanna-Sin: The Moon - "Who Shines For" … 106

   2—Nabu-Tutu: Mercury - "Who Speaks For" … 113

   3—Inanna-Ishtar: Venus - "Queen of Heaven" … 118

   4—Shammash: The Sun - "Shinning One" … 125

   5—Nergal & Ereshkigal: Mars & The Shadowlands … 132

   6—Marduk: Jupiter - "King of the Gods" … 140

   7—Ninib-Ninurta:
      Saturn - "Who Completes the Foundation" … 147

APPENDIX

A—Mesopotamian Mathematics:
Secrets of Measuring Space and Time ... 157

B—Mardukite Sigil-Seals of the Anunnaki:
"*Necronomicon: The Anunnaki Bible*" (*Tablet X*) ... 161

C—The Book of Marduk by Nabu:
"*Necronomicon : The Anunnaki Bible*" (*Tablet W*) ... 172

D—Ladder of Lights:
Initiations of the Ancient Mystery Schools ... 181

E—Enuma Eliš:
The Babylonian Epic of Creation ... 185

Index ... 196

MARDUKITE CHAMBERLAINS

—PART ONE—
ANCIENT MESOPOTAMIA

— 0 —
ESOTERIC ASSYRIOLOGY OF THE 21ST CENTURY

> *"When the sculptures and huge, dramatic bas-reliefs from Babylon and Nineveh, uncovered by the excavations of Layard and Rawlinson in the mid-19th century, began to arrive in Europe, the people were enthralled but they were also fickle. The greater accessibility of Egypt, and the sheer quantity of the material excavated and exported, pushed Babylon and Assyria into the background, and the civilizations of the Tigris and the Euphrates began to be perceived as colorless and dull, even by esotericists."*
> ~ R.A. Gilbert, Foreword
> L.W. King's *Babylonian Magic & Sorcery*

Mystics of every age go forth explaining an almost *quantum* vision of reality and existence: entangled, interconnected—*All-as-One*. While this might seem a truly obscure approach to crossing the current threshold of what is typically deemed an "academic" topic; it is not. Consider for a moment that our *mythic past* is very much rooted in *truth*—albeit misunderstood but a *truth* that has been conveniently, or forcefully, forgotten among mass awareness.

Politics and the general *human condition* evolving outside of the *Ancient Mystery School* have, throughout history, taken its toll on accounts of said *truth*, as becomes quite evident concerning the history of the geographic region known as *Mesopotamia*.

Humans, accepting a *mortal* paradigm, are unaware of one critical aspect of the cosmos—one that they can not see based on limited perceptions and reality experiences schematized by semantic labeling—that *Universal Truth* is actually *unchanging*. Some have even put forth to call it "Cosmic Law."

In spite of the best (or worst) human efforts across time, the *Truth* has survived to remind us of our origins, to instruct us on where we have to go and perhaps, most importantly, the standards we should live by to get there. Mere survival of *Secret Doctrines* by select cabals is not enough. For as the world was once plummeted into *Dark Ages* only to be *reincarnated* in an *Age of Enlightenment*, the "esoteric" *truth* did not resurface in public "exoteric" consciousness—in fact, it went the other direction: *underground* and into *vaults* of obscure "occult" factions.

Original and intended meaning behind esoteric symbolism, used to preserve the integrity of *mysteries*, became as confounded and obscure to mystical practitioners and "magicians" as the nature of their own organizations. What's more: they *convinced* themselves that they *did* have true comprehension of it—and so, eventually, politics reflecting the surface world became no less existent in the underground. As above; so below ...*apparently*.

Quests to satisfy an innate desire to pursue *truth*, particularly what has been known as the *Secret of the Ages*, are as obvious in realms of science and academia as they are in the world of the occultist. "Esotericists" are not the only ones interested in unearthing these matters, nor are they even the original ones. Only the methodologies and intentions differ. And yet again— all is connected.

Without intellectual and scholarly pursuits by historians and academicians, we might have far fewer clues to reconstruct our *mental image* of the past. Where then would the *truth seeker* turn to draw inspiration? From fanciful distortions of pantheism and anthropomorphic fairy-tales passed around by the uninitiated? Certainly, not.

Recovery of the *truth* of mankind's past is paramount to understanding humanity's destined future. It should come as no surprise then that the geographical region associated with its origins remains victim to unyielding war and suffering for thousands of years—further enshrouding our efforts to unveil with a patina of public hesitation and doubt painted by political opinions toward modern *Middle East* activity. For our current esoteric purposes, focus is restricted to what academicians call the *Ancient Near East* —or *Mesopotamia*.

For over a century, modern pursuit of the *Great Babylonian Mysteries* remained primarily restricted to two approaches: Firstly, the late 19th century archaeological excavations inspiring academic Exoteric Assyriology; and the Second, derived from the same, made crude esoteric attempts at reviving a working understanding. In the first, no attempt is made at philosophical or mystical pragmatism; the entire field of study left as dry as the desert sands it is drawn from. In the second, early works of these stoic academicians are used at face value to base a revival mystical tradition—often giving little regard for *specifics* of the *system* and effectively requiring many additional facets of knowledge directly appearing nowhere on the same fractured clay tablets and artifacts excavated from these ancient sites.

Fortunately, the 21st century *truth seeker* has a *third* option to explore.

In 2008, a revolutionary esoteric underground organization known as the "Mardukites" appeared, publicly visible, and a completely new breed of *next generation* "Esoteric Assyriologists" emerged on the scene—one that would not blindly accept the given data from their predecessors—at least not at *face value*.

For over a decade this diversely organized research group sought out the most ancient writings rendered on clay tablets from *Babylonia*—now available to the public as a complete collection in Joshua Free's *"Necronomicon: The Anunnaki Bible."* These writings demonstrate an integral link directly between our origins and the remaining evolution of human civilization. Our chosen method and the resulting clarity revealed concerning the identity, nature and progression of this *incredible* subject matter show undeniable superiority to what was previously available. But, that is what we call *progress* (much needed for this field).

The *Mardukite* approach to reconstructing the *Babylonian* vision begins with first revealing the incredible misnomer that the field of study has endured far too long, for essentially, the applicable term "Assyriology" is a lie. It is not even semantically correct for our current pursuits of *analysis* using the same physical *evidences* brought to light by late 19th and early 20th century archeology. The name questionably applies to the field at all! And although some early scholars acknowledge this grave misrepresentation of the science, it has as yet gone unchallenged in contemporary academics.

George G. Cameron explains in his foreword to Edward Chiera's *"They Wrote on Clay"* (1938): "Few there are indeed who know that the name of our science, 'Assyriology' is based on an accident—the fact that the first large group of texts ever discovered were written in Assyrian. Assyrian itself is but one dialect." Misapplication arises with use of the term to denote study of any and all ancient cuneiform-using cultures. Mardukites do not propagate this blatant disregard for the political and spiritual history of Mesopotamia. Although cuneiform-literate and sharing a similar "Anunnaki" tradition, the Assyrians were actually northwestern foreigners to Babylon. The two are not the same.

As previously mentioned, any true esoteric analysis or mystical application are absent from the earliest academic-archaeological pursuits. These efforts mainly emphasized the *recovery* and *accumulation* of translatable materials, much of which are not yet coherently transliterated into English language even a century after their discovery. Most materials readily available to *seekers* during the *pre-mardukite* era of research and development are severely fragmented, confounding itself in the information relay.

Earliest attempts at understanding ancient Mesopotamia made by "Assyriologists" of the late 19th and 20th century, included: E.A. Budge, Edward Chiera, L.W. King, S.L. Noah Kramer, Franqois Lenormant, R.C. Thompson and L.A. Waddell. Their renderings have already received long-standing public attention for those who sought it. The variegated cultural influences and often violent history of *Babylonia* has left a confusion of names, titles and images that have required over a century to flush out to any practical ends, by scholars and mystics alike.

Origins for the field-name of *"Assyriology"* are derived from French excavations at the city ruins of *Khorsabad, Nimrud, Nineveh, Sippar* and *Lagash* (*Telloh*) in the 1840's. However, a true scientific pursuit was ignited when the royal library archives of the Assyrian king *Assurbanipal* were discovered. Thousands of clues, in the form of cuneiform tablet writings, illuminated a prehistoric legacy formerly thought of as completely forgotten and never again salvageable.

Then, in the 1880's, German archaeologists unearthed *Babylon...*

— 1 —
: MESOPOTAMIAN MYSTERIES :
BEFORE BABYLON – THE LAND OF SUMER

> *"Here [in Babylon] is real death. Not a column or arch still stands to demonstrate the permanency of human work. Everything has crumbled to dust. The very temple tower, the most imposing of all these ancient constructions, has entirely lost its shape. Where are now its seven stages? We see nothing but a mound of earth – all that remains of the millions of its bricks. Here the ancient mysteries and their tombs have been sleeping quietly for millenniums. In a few months, perhaps in a few days, the ground will be broken by trenches as in a battlefield. And the repose of the poor dead will be disturbed by the frantic search for records and data..."*
> ~ Edward Chiera, *"They Wrote On Clay"*
> *From a letter to his wife*

Before Babylon—when history had not yet been written—the land now known to modern man as the "Middle East" was first occupied by "gods" of antiquity—the *Anunnaki*. These super-human figures molded and shaped human consciousness and the systematized civilization we so easily take for granted in the "Western World" today. The wheel of time forced the age of "gods" to become an era of "men" and *their* ways, but the ancient foundations built in Mesopotamia remain strong among us today.

Classical period Greeks may be credited with the term: *Mesopotamia*—meaning "A land between two rivers." More literal than poetic, the title accurately describes thre region known to the ancients as *Babylonia*—the "Land of the Gates of the Gods" and the "City of Star-Gates" established primarily between two rivers—the *Tigris* and the *Euphrates*. Today, the term *Babylonia* is used to distinguish post-Sumerian *empires* maintained by *Babylonian* kings, a lineage made famous by Hammurabi, the powerful "Mardukite" systematizer of Babylon.

Commonly compared to the fertile Nile region of Egypt, *Mesopotamia* is also a river-delta system—and, like the Nile to the Egyptians, this system of life-giving waters proved to be inseparable from prosperity of the people. The plain was cultivated successfully by use of the first "aqueduct-irrigation" systems. Accurate construction and upkeep of these canals were vital to keep *Babylonia* habitable in all seasons.

Eventually, as they were abandoned under foreign control, dissolution of the aqueduct system resulted in complete collapse of *Babylon* as the "throne of the earth" and the lands returned to the indistinct sand they were born from.

Ancient Mesopotamia is famous for its original inhabitants—those who occupied the area before, and reestablished it after, a "Great Flood"—"Uruk" Sumerians and "Akkadian" Babylonians (and then later Assyrians); indigenous folk calling their native land *kengir*—meaning "local." The proto-Sumerian "Ubaid" launched the first primary post-diluvian Mesopotamian cities: *Eridu, Ur, Isin, Larsa, Lagash, Nippur* and *Uruk* (also known as *Erech* and possibly the origins of the name *Iraq*), all situated on established foundations from a former age.

Charting exact political boundaries of *Babylonia* is difficult. They are not generally agreed upon—no more today among scholars and nationalists then by those who once physically fought for them in periods of antiquity. For as long as humans have been involved, the area has been plagued with constant conflict. Mesopotamian territory often included areas beyond the pathway of the two rivers, which even themselves changed positions and course over time with alteration (and then absence) by human intervention.

Ancient *Babylonia* essentially occupies present-day Iraq, in a region bordered by mountains separating it (on the east) from Iran; ancient Persia. To the south, the empire once extended to the Persian Gulf where the archetypal city of *Eridu* was founded. On the western front, Mesopotamia is separated from the Mediterranean and Magan-Egypt (Khem) by the vast expanse of Arabian desert, and just north of this: the land of Syria.

The full expanse of the "Ancient Near East" includes geographical locations now occupied as Iran, Iraq, Saudi Arabia, Yemen, Oman, Lebanon, Israel, Syria and the United Arab Emirates. Mesopotamian kingdoms also included (at some time or another) occupations in modern-day Turkey, Armenia, Afghanistan, Pakistan, Egypt and Sudan.

The modern term "Middle East" is a Euro-centric political semantic replacing academic usage of the "Near East," as opposed to the "Far East" or "oriental." With few exceptions, the Ancient Near East and its *Anunnaki* legacy is the direct origin of most major world religions in history, including (but not limited to) Zoroastrianism (Mazdaism), Mithraism, Canaanite, Yezidism (Yazdanism), Baha'i Faith, Manichaeism (Mandaeism), Islam, Judaism and Christianity.

The legendary city of Babylon stood alongside the western-laying of the two rivers, the *Euphrates* (in the Greek language) called *burannon* or *perath* by the Sumerians (and *puratu* by the Assyrian Babylonians)—all meaning simply "river." It is considerably longer of the two rivers—at 1,800 miles—forming first in the heights of the mountains at 11,000 feet above sea level. It quickly drops off then falls approximately one foot per mile for the last 1,200 miles of its run. The pathway taken by the river has consistently moved westward with the absence of human intervention and canals—creating more area "between" the rivers. The water levels are indicative of the equinoxes, like the Egyptian Nile, with the *Euphrates* rising in the spring and lowering in the autumn – though unlike the Nile, which is altered by the summer monsoon season, the levels of the *Euphrates* river peaks in the springtime.

Opposite the *Euphrates*, the broad eastern river runs 1,150 miles and, like the other, the path has also shifted to what archeologists believe to be its more 'natural' flow with the abandonment of the irrigation canals. The Greeks pronounce the Assyrian name for the river as *Tigris*, essentially meaning "*serpent river*" (*i-di-ik-lat*) although the original Sumerian identification meant "*fast as an arrow*" (*idigna* or *id-dagal-la*). Babylonians found the *Tigris* to be too wild to cross easily or irrigate with. The water levels also rise and fall in direct opposition to the cycle of the *Euphrates*. Ancient cities founded alongside (and making use of) the *Tigris River* include *Nineveh, Calah (Nimrud)* and *Asshur*.

Before emptying into the Persian Gulf, the *Euphrates* and *Tigris* join together forming a marshy delta region called the "Great Swamp." The prehistoric city of *Eridu* was once a lavish capital there, at the coast of the Persian Gulf. Today, however, ruins and remains of *Eridu* now rest 130 miles away from the sea. This shift over time is attributed to a "shrinking" Persian Gulf, creating more land—approximately *72 feet* of it *per* year!

"E-RI-DU" [*House in the Distance, Built*] is the original Mesopotamian home of the Anunnaki god ENKI—a prototype-city of *Babylon* built prior to the "Great Flood," then later rebuilt, ever remaining the sacred precinct of ENKI in *Babylonia*. It is the oldest capital city of the proto-Uruk Sumerians, dated to over seven-thousand years ago. Its remains are found at *Tell abu Shahrain* (Arabic name).

It is in *Eridu*, that the modern practices of "ceremonial" and religious "magic" (or "magick" if you prefer) are also born. The Anunnaki god MARDUK and his demigod son NABU both apprenticed there, learning the esoteric and intellectual sciences from ENKI.

The Ubaid-Sumerians or proto-Sumerians occupied Mesopotamia before the Uruk-Sumerians—origins of what we call the *historical* "Enlilite Sumerians" from a period of at least the Fifth Millennium B.C. The name designation (*"Ubaid"*) comes only from modern archaeological excavation of ruins at *Tell Ubaid*—a primitive city built near the area later established as the Uruk-Sumerian city of Ur. True urban systematization became present during Uruk occupation and was later perfected by the Babylonians, who inspired Empire-builders forever thereafter.

Distinct natural terrain separate Mesopotamia into northern and southern parts; a factor long exploited for political purposes to define boundaries. Originally, southern *Sumer* (Also called *Sumeria, Shinar, Babili, Babylonia* or *Chaldea* in varying texts) and northern *Akkad* each were ruled by their own governors, called a *patesi*. [Modern "Mardukites" retained usage of the title to indicate a priest/minister-bishop of a particular region or diocese.] A post-Sumerian unification of the two lands and rise of the *Babylonian Empire* led to replacing this role with the *lugal*—a title applied to the *"Mighty King of both Sumer & Akkad"*—Literally: *lu*—man; *gal*—great or lofty. The "Big Man"—*The King*.

The northern half of Mesopotamia was once forested and so it retains features of prairie and plains mixed with a mountainous supply of stones and crystals. The southern part is naturally more barren, primarily swamps and marshes mixed with arid desert. Without the aid of an incredible irrigation system, the *Babylonian Empire* would never have had the freedom and sustainability to survive and flourish as the spiritual and political epicenter of the ancient world.

The ever-changing shape of the land was once expertly engineered to meet the needs of an awe-inspiring unparalleled civilization. Proper cultivation of the land was the original key—making societal life possible among humans, and of this knowledge they attributed to the *gods*— great beings who taught the people how to shape the land and launch city-life to sustain their own livelihood on earth. With the 'land between the rivers' prepared and consecrated, *kingship* could now be *lowered* from *heaven*.

— 2 —
: SARGON & THE SUMERIANS :
DIVINE RIGHT IN THE LAND OF SUMER

An examination of the Sumerian and Babylonian King-Lists will reveal the belief that "kingship" was "sent down" from "heaven" as decreed by the gods. To this we might add that a similar tradition has been followed by many indigenous ancient cultures. These dynastic lists originate by Sumerian hands, but the were later recatalogued in Babylon by Nabu Priest-Scribes. Similar King-Lists have also been found in Egypt and they all suggest some very amazing notions for the contemporary mind to grasp.
~ Joshua Free
From the original Liber-51

"Divine Right" to reign on earth "lowered down" from the "heavens" to *Eridu*—but "kingship" moved. Prior to the establishment of *Mardukite Babylon*, most Uruk-Sumerian activity concentrated in southern parts of Mesopotamia. *Eridu*—the home of ENKI—becomes a secondary capital when Sumerian cultural and "religious" emphasis develops in the *Enlilite* city of *Uruk* (also called *Erech*). To establish *Uruk* as a capital *holy city* in the consciousness of Sumerians, the national *ziggurat* temple-shrine of ANU, the E-ANNA, was built there to accommodate rare appearances made by the highest *Anunnaki* Divine Couple—ANU and ANTU—on earth. This *ziggurat* was later "gifted" to the Anunnaki goddess INANNA-ISHTAR, from which she based her own worldly rule.

Kingship is central to establishing "societal systems," forming the basis of Sumerian and Babylonian lore and all paradigms born from the Anunnaki (traditions). Examination of ancient *King-Lists* from Mesopotamia reveals an archaic premise that "kingship" was *brought down* or *sent down* from the "heavens" as decreed by the gods. Of course, the idea of *monarchy* or kingship was not always executed by humans to the highest regard; misuse of these systems leads to their inevitable breakdown.

The complete text of the cuneiform *King-Lists* is found as the Tablet-K Series in *"Necronomicon: The Anunnaki Bible."* The oldest example in Sumerian language is the *Weld-Blundell Prism*. These records were later adapted by Babylonian scribes and then by the classical Historian Berossus in the 3rd Century B.C. A similar chronicle was prepared around the same time for Egypt by the Historian Manetho.

Chronology of the *King-Lists* are separated by a critical event, one found within cosmological records of all ancient cultures—the *Deluge* or *Great Flood*. This means that Sumerian civilization actually began in *antediluvian* times, prior to the *Deluge*. The *King-Lists* are consistent with this time scale too, but the shifting sands of Mesopotamia provide us few direct clues. Ancient sites were often dismantled or found in ruins and later built over by cultural successors. What this signifies is that the pre-Babylonian, pre-Sumerian *Ubaid* periods are not the true absolute origins for this prehistoric civilization, but instead are origins for civilized efforts resumed after the earth was stable for societal habitation again, probably following the last Ice Age.

Ancient writings do not dispute that a pre-Sumerian "civilizations" and other Anunnaki "experiments" have come and gone on the planet. Archeologists can successfully confirm identities of the *King-Lists* until c. 3200 B.C., yet these records continue into the past for another 420,000+ years.

Sumerian and Egyptian records are very clear about the nature of the beings occupying seats of kingship at its inception—*gods*. Original *overseers* were considered *divine*, thought to have come from the stars/sky and bringing with them the knowledge and technologies that could cultivate humanity. Reign of these *divine* beings was eventually replaced by *hybrid demigods* (part-*Divine*; part-*human*) until finally passed to control of a specialized segment—*Royal Blood*—of mankind. Hybrid offspring of gods as kings were *demigods*, which required both parents to be 'divine', but the offspring could be born on earth. "Part-" or "half-" divine 'kings' later emerging in the population required only one 'divine' or 'demigod' parent.

ANCIENT LIFESPANS ON THE KING-LISTS

"Divine" = *10,000's* of years old
"Demigod" = *1,000's* of years old
"Deity/Hero" = *100's* of yeas old

god + god = demigod (*"divine"*)
demigod + god = demigod (*"lordly"*)
god + human = deity (*"half-divine"*)
demigod + human = deity (*"half-divine"*)
deity + human = hero (*"quarter-breed"*)

At each stage of development, the concept of *dynastic succession* remains paramount—the idea that "Divine Blood" flows from the heart of *true* kings in the lineage, which in turn may be passed on to their offspring. The tradition of *Divine Right to Rule* is as ancient as human society altogether and may even have origins beyond only this planet. Cosmological tablets illuminate a similar tradition of *Divine Succession* practiced by the *Anunnaki* ("sky gods")—particularly ANU, ENLIL and ENKI—describing control of heavenly domains and celestial zones.

Origins of the word "ruler," "regent" and "realm" all reflect the perceived "god-like" nature of the original "King" role. After the unification of the two lands of Mesopotamia, one hero-man—one *lugal*—was elevated to the position of a blessed and lofty *demigod*. More than simply a title of power, this role required the person to be an active intermediary between the people and the *gods* and thus acted as a powerful *priest-king*.

Interconnectedness between the "realm" and the king was inseparable. The king and his land are one. The king and his people are one. The fate of one has proved to reflect in the other throughout history and populations couldn't deny observing it—a good and just king resulted in social expansion and a fruitful land, whereas rule of unjust ungodly tyrants weakened the integrity of the *Babylonian Empire* every time.

Properly guided kings realized they were essentially a *Divine Representation* on earth and with this came great responsibility. In fact, the freedoms, responsibilities and penalties of Mesopotamian society all *rose* relative with class—quite different even, than what we see often today. The 'true' kings understood that they existed *for* the people, representatives of the *gods* on earth, exercising a *divine power* reflecting the *gods* themselves during the cultivation of the "human condition."

Descent of kingship came from the *gods of heaven* themselves, but is carried in the hearts of men—passed on as genetic memory. Recognition of "Divine Blood" conjured a system known as *jure divino*—the episcopal law (from the Greek *episkopos*, meaning "overseer") upheld by an individual "anointed" or "chosen" by *God*.

> *"I am Sargon, the Mighty King of Akkad.*
> *MARDUK smiled upon me,*
> *And by his love, I was made a ruler of the kingdom."*
> —The Sargon Tablet

Sargon of Akkad (*Sharru-Kin*)—also called Sargon-the-Great—is sometimes confused by amateur researchers with another later Babylonian king sharing the same name, Sargon II, an Assyrian who appears on the scene nearly two-thousand years afterward during the *Neo-Babylonian Empire*. Sargon is the first "Babylonian" King to reign supreme over all of the lands in Mesopotamia. He is founder of the Akkadian dynasty and the archetypal World Emperor, but was also the first *Mardukite King*—a chosen chamberlain, blessed by the Anunnaki god MARDUK, patron deity of *Babylon*. A chaotic anti-Sumerian hold on the land by a pre-Babylonian tribe called the Umma was relinquished in c. 2600 B.C. by Sargon. [Although texts developed by scribes of Nabunidus—known as the "long chronology"—indicate this time as c. 3750 BC.]

Similar to the story of Moses, Sargon is the bastard son of a priestess. He is placed in a reed basket and floated down a river, found, then raised by the *King of Kish*. He grows up to overthrow the king and declares himself supreme in *Akkad* and then setting his sights on *Sumer*—the campaign for a southern Mesopotamian takeover ensues, beginning with the city of *Uruk*. His sophisticated military operations coupled with a weights and measures standardization allowed unified organization of the first "world empire."

Sargon's son Rimush (c. 2580 B.C.) reigned after his father's death, becoming the self-proclaimed *King of Kish*—a title which cost him his life. After his murder, his brother Manishtusu replaced him, during which another tribe, the Elamites, revolt. His son, Naram-Sin, named himself the *King of the Four Quarters* and successfully conquered the Magan lands located on the Arabian peninsula, separating Mesopotamia from Egypt. He wrongfully did so in the tradition of the Enlilite *Anunnaki gods*—rejecting his Mardukite heritage—and as punishment for supporting a neo-Sumerian Renaissance, the rapid expansion caused the heart of a once-Mardukite global empire to weaken...*for a time*.

— 3 —
: SIFTING SUMERIAN SANDS :
UNEARTHING THE ANUNNAKI LEGACY OF KINGS

> *"Since Marduk created me to be king and Nabu has culled his people to my realm – as the love I have for my own life, so do I feel toward the building and reign of their cities."*
> ~ King Nebuchadnezzar II
> The Mardukite Tablet-L Series
> *"Necronomicon: The Anunnaki Bible"*

The Akkadian Dynasty of Sargon began in northern Mesopotamia—in the land of Akkad. Akkadian territory and influence was of only tribal significance during the early rise of Sumerians proper, but when Sargon used his military to unify the "two lands" of Mesopotamia, he established the first post-Sumerian empire in the world. Indeed, for the first time, lands of *Akkad* and *Sumer* were governed from a single capital: Sargon's city of *Agade* (the city of *Akkad* in the land of *Akkad*, like *Babylon* in *Babylonia* or *New York, New York*), a city named after the word "unity" in Akkadian language.

As a culture and language, Akkadian evolved alongside, but separate, from the southern Sumerians. It is fortunate, however, that they were participants in the same Celestial *Anunnaki* tradition. Akkadians possessed their own distinct proto-Semitic culture and language, but shared the Sumerian dedication to an *Anunnaki* "pantheon" and also used a refined version of cuneiform 'wedge-styled' writing to represent their own language, which replaced the Sumerian *emegir* mother-tongue. Akkadian language also evolved separately as other Semitic languages, like Hebrew, Canaanite, Phoenician, Arabic and Aramaic.

Assimilation of many pre-Babylonian (Sumerian) "programs" and Enlilite "systems" permitted a social transition into post-Sumerian or "Mardukite" ideologies. This energetic change and paradigm-shift in human consciousness occurred simultaneously as humanity entered the astrological Age of Aries in 2160 B.C. Several Sumerian literary cycles (cuneiform tablet series) are retained almost verbatim—inscribed by a new order of scribes, magician-priests and priestesses using Akkadian language. For example: *Inanna-Ishtar's Descent into the Underworld* and the *Epic of Gilgamesh* are both of purely Sumerian (pre-Babylonian) origin. Versions simply remained existent in Babylonian libraries.

This new (post-Sumerian) Babylonian-Akkadian literary and religious tradition shifted its emphasis from an Enlilite "World Order" to one in dedication of MARDUK. The "Mardukite Legacy" replaces the old paradigm altogether. Although the actual identities of the Supernal Trinity (ANU, ENLIL and ENKI) and Anunnaki pantheon already established remain, the emphasis turns to the "younger generation" of Anunnaki, best represented in Babylonian Tradition.

THE ANUNNAKI "SUPERNAL TRINITY"

ANU—the *distant* "Father" in *heaven* who birthed and "commanded" the Anunnaki gods visiting earth.
ENLIL—the *local* "Father" in the *skies* who established the Sumerian "World Order" of Anunnaki gods of earth.
ENKI—the *patron* "Father" on *earth* who maintains all Anunnaki "systems" and cosmic "programs" of existence.

The new Babylonian vision heralded the new god MARDUK as a local patron deity of *Babylon*. This replaced the more primitive rural ideals of Sumerian life with systematized urbanization that humans continue to live in the shadows of. All these new traditions attributed to MARDUK and *Babylon* were inherited from his *Anunnaki* father, ENKI—magic and wisdom, sciences and religion; these become central to city community infrastructure.

In pre-Babylonian *Sumer*, ENKI assisted his brother ENLIL in the development of the *cosmos*—the organization of physical worldly systems (or 'world order'). ENKI is given domain of the physical sciences, mathematics and esoteric magic. Among the "Race of Marduk" (*Mardukite Babylonians*), ENKI is sometimes referred to as "Our Father." This arm of the Supernal Trinity is shared with his espoused consort NINKI, also known as DAMKINA.

By earlier Sumerian standards during the Age of Taurus (c.4200-2160 B.C.), ENLIL is the heir to *"Anuship"* in *"Heaven"*—the position of "God" for the local universe. Later duality observed in the Babylonian pantheon between lineages of ENKI and ENLIL occurred 'on earth as it is in heaven'. ANU, by name and title, is the "Father in Heaven," the All-Father to the *gods*—but particularly the biological parent to both ENKI and ENLIL.

Most of Sargon's immediate descendents did not possess his same integrity when he first conducted his world building campaign—even as militant as he was. His dynasty was soon replaced by the Enlilite Gutians in c. 2450 B.C. When their reign in Mesopotamia was rejected, confusion swept over the region until an acceptable dynasty was established.

The new dynasty came again from Lagash. Of the *patesi* in that line the most influential include Urbau, who expanded the cult-power of the E.NINNU in Lagash as well as many other religious centers. Then, King Gudea cultivated further abundance and economic prosperity by opening and securing trade routes.

With the death of Gudea's son, Ur-Dingirsu, no proper heir was brought forth and the dynastic line ended (c. 2250 B.C.) allowing the "seat of power" to be passed back to the old Sumerian city (and "Third Dynasty") of *Ur*, led by Ur-Engur (Ur-Nammu) who focused on the fortification of the Babylonian infrastructure, but with a reinstatement of the former "glory" of ENLIL and the "Old Ways." His son, Dungi (better known as Shulgi), called himself the *High Priest* of ANU when he began to reinforce significance of the *Eridu* site and the legacy of ENKI. But there is much more to this part of the story.

The patron deity of the famous Sumerian city, *Ur*, is the *Anunnaki god* NANNA (called SIN by the Babylonians, meaning "moon"). A long-standing Enlilite patronage to NANNA-SIN in *Ur* was maintained as payment for a "life-debt owed," when the *god* personally arranged the marriage between Ur-Nammu and "a high priestess of the Temple of Ur." In the balance of this, the dynasty of Ur sought a truly 'Sumerian' Renaissance, which fought hard to thwart any advancement of the Mardukites. [This prestigious city is remembered in biblical accounts as "*Ur of the Chaldeans.*"]

Shulgi (Dungi) continued efforts toward an anti-Mardukite "Sumerian Renaissance" ushered in by his father's pact with NANNA-SIN. Economic and agricultural abundance was found under his reign, but uprisings and social rebellions sparked by this "new" Mardukite movement grew rather than diminished. Shulgi became a "lover" to the Enlilite *Anunnaki goddess queen* INANNA-ISHTAR, and under her blessing began fighting newly formed "Nabu-tribes" (ancient Mardukites) in 2095 B.C. This continuing even after the mathematical shift to the Age of Aries—a task he passed down to his son, Amar-Sin (*A.Mar-Su.en*—"Son of the Moon God"), a warlord king who unleashed vengeance on all (Mardukite) rebels. The "Great War" ensued between 2048 and 2024 B.C., resulting in unleashed nuclear weapons (born of *alien* knowledge) against these pro-Mardukite westerners, the *Amorites*.

Akkadians knew of this group evolving on the outskirts of their Semitic lineage—the *Amurru* (Sumerian – *A.Mar-Tu*). This unique culture and language developed independent of the Sumerians, centralized around the cult-city center of Mari, west of the Euphrates, often referred to in lore as the "*Land of Martu*" (*Amar* to the Egyptians). Much like other Mardukite efforts in Enlilite territory, the Judeo-Christian biblical accounts reflect a harsh bias towards these "Canaanites" stating in the *Book of Jubilees* (called the *Leptogenesis*) that: "The former giants, the *Rephaim*, gave way to the *Amorites*, an evil and sinful people whose wickedness surpasses that of any other, and whose life will be cut short on the earth."

Development of early Amorite ("Mardukite") culture contributed not only to the collapse of the *Ur III* Dynasty, but also to the founding of *Babylon* as a proper city-state and the division of Sumerian Mesopotamia into republic-styled Amorite Kingdoms, a system that remained primarily in effect for at least four centuries, from 2100 B.C. to 1700 B.C. These Amorite tribes first began forming in Mari (Syria) and Canaan around 2400 B.C. In biblical literature, "Amorite" and "Canaanite" appear synonymous. Three hundred years later (c. 2112 B.C.) the Amorites arrived onto the Mesopotamian scene during the confusion and chaos following the fall of the Akkadian Empire. These nomadic hunter-gatherers, once preferring temporary shanty towns and tents over Enlilite Sumerian city life, began to adopt agriculture, homesteading and assimilated native Mesopotamian cultural systems as they re-stabilized the post-Sumerian world of *Babylonia*. Various kingdoms were established throughout the lands. Multiple city-states observed their own Amorite Dynasties, but only one would be responsible for launching a true Mardukite Empire—Hammurabi, famous King of Babylon.

— 4 —
: CODES OF HAMMURABI :
BUILDING BABYLON AND BEYOND

"Whereas Sargon seems to have relied upon his power and his terror tactics to keep people under control, Hammurabi presents himself almost like a modern politician in that he wants to be loved; he wants the people to like him; he's going to set up laws that will protect them, not laws that will terrify them or force them into submission."
~ Amanda Podany
California State Polytech, Pomona

In the post-Sumerian "Mardukite" era of Mesopotamia, Anunnaki traditions and systems were sealed under MARDUK, heir-son of ENKI. During this shift to the Age of Aries—the sign of MARDUK, represented by the Ram—"divine politics" fueled religion, spirituality and the global reality experience. The famous "creation stories" and "esoteric symbolism," serving basis for all future traditions and societal reality systems, were forged onto cuneiform tablets of quasi-propaganda supporting a 'Babylonian' paradigm by the priest-scribes of ('led by' or 'dedicated to') NABU, heir of MARDUK.

The "Younger Generation" of Anunnaki become figures central to the structure of Mardukite Babylonian systems. These traditions are a direct evolution of the previous Sumerian legacy. It charts progression of a particular Anunnaki "family" in Mesopotamia and is not simply an arbitrary assimilation or recreation, as evident in similar "Celestial" pantheons found elsewhere in "classical mythology."

Long after the vision put forth by Sargon, the next most famous and influential contributor to a "Mardukite Babylon" in Mesopotamia was King Hammurabi (1790 B.C. by the short chronology). In homage of MARDUK's own legacy put forth in the '*Enuma Elis*' (the "*Epic of Creation*" text given fully in "*Necronomicon: The Anunnaki Bible*"), King Hammurabi reconstructed the *ziggurat* temple-shrine and earth-home of the Anunnaki god MARDUK, the E.SAG-ILA. The structure was once built in even more remote times in an attempt to establish a Mardukite "World Order" prematurely during Mesopotamia's early evolution – an effort brought down by the Enlilite Sumerians in the archetypal fall of the "Tower of Babel."

The region around *Babylon* hosted human occupation since at least the Third Millennium B.C. (the period of Sargon of Akkad around 2300 B.C.). That being said, the independent *Babylonian* city-state of the "Mardukite" legacy we know today was invigorated primarily by efforts from the Amorite Dynasty; specifically Hammurabi, who goes on to replace the former Enlilite Sumerian tradition in total with a complete Mardukite Babylonian establishment.

Under the reign of Hammurabi, Sumerian language became denationalized and scribes began recording all literature in the "new" Akkadian (Old Babylonian) language. This literary tradition accounts for many pre-Assyrian era tablets of Babylonia found and translated today.

Most importantly—this Babylonian literary revolution allowed a means to evolve a firmly rooted Anunnaki tradition with an emphasis on MARDUK as the supreme "King of the Gods"—thus completely replacing the previously accepted Sumerian paradigm.

King Hammurabi is considered the greatest empire engineer since Sargon of Akkad, and in many ways was culturally and spiritually superior. Efforts conducted during his forty-two year reign allowed a centralized 'world government' of *Babylon* to form that not only served the people on an emotional, cultural and religio-spiritual level, but also reaching record-breaking energetic and monetary heights in global wealth, power and influence. Ruling in honor of MARDUK allowed Hammurabi to bring *Babylon* to fruition with cultural and spiritual heights that would not be visited again for at least a millennium—the Neo-Babylonian era of Nebuchadnezzar II.

Of the many conventions and systems first introduced to human civilization from *Babylon,* Hammurabi's legal code is one of the most significant to note —made popular in mass-consciousness as the *"eye for an eye"* methodology, but best known simply as the "Code of Hammurabi." While tyrannical and draconian penalties are the most frequently cited examples of the "Code," details of the 282 laws established, for the first time, a complete methodology of citizen rights, property rights, social rights and even feminine equality rights in addition to the creation of a "class" system.

The "Code of Hammurabi," by its own account, does not even originate from Hammurabi's own mind. He considered himself merely a catalyst for the reign and power of something *greater* than himself—that of the patron deity, MARDUK. The "Code" or Law of Hammurabi, is what modern Mardukites call the *"Book of the Law of Marduk."*

The Mardukite source book anthology—"*Necronomicon: The Anunnaki Bible*"—relays *The Book of the Law of Marduk* as it was given to the race of Dragonblood Kings—those who ruled in the name of MARDUK on Earth. Priests, priestesses and priest-kings of *Babylon* ruled by a covenant: the descent of kingship on Earth from Heaven in honor of MARDUK who granted freedom for men to rule in Mesopotamia as in Egypt. They did so in his name. And often took on his name and the name of his family members during their reign. But, after Khammurabi's death, invasion by the Hittites broke this Babylonian dynasty, followed by a series of mysterious "sea-kings" that eventually spawn a second Babylonian dynasty: the *Kassites*.

— 5 —
: THE KASSITE DYNASTY :
PRESERVING A LEGACY OF LEGENDS

"The Hittite Empire spread over all of Antolia and parts of Syria and north Mesopotamia, including regions of different background, culturally, ethically & linguistically, including Sumerian & Akkadian."
~ Hans G. Guterbock
The Art & Literature of the Hittites

When the *Old Babylonian* age ended, loose social organization and a broken political system left the empire open for a new dynastic power change. Fortunately for *Babylon*, a pro-Marduk force known as the Kassites (c. 1750 B.C.) came down from the Zagros Mountain region northeast of *Babylonia*. Kassite culture assimilated MARDUK with their own deity-name, *Shuqamuna* (possibly from *Shakyamuni*, meaning "Buddha"). They defended *Mardukite Babylon* against years of struggle with the Hittites who sought to claim *Babylonia* for themselves.

In 1595 B.C. (some sources suggest 1651 B.C. depending on chronology), the Hittites successfully enter Babylon and "steal" MARDUK. Historians usually interpret this to mean that they *"removed the image of Marduk"* from the temple—the main statue or *idol* representing the 'seat of power' in Babylon. Others might conclude that the Anunnaki god himself was actually captured while still residing on earth. In either case, the Kassites devoted over two decades in battle toward recovering and returning the *"idol"* to the temple. Overcoming tremendous struggles against the Hittites, by the grace of MARDUK, the Kassite Dynasty established its own reign of *Babylon*, with few minor exceptions, for nearly half a millennium.

Kassites were a diplomatic people, enjoying trade relations with most of the known world, including Egypt, which was undergoing a spiritual revolution under the rule of Amonhotep IV (1350 B.C.), better known as Akhenaton. This new pharaoh changed the face of Egypt by installing his "Mardukite" *Marduk-Aten-Ra Star-Religion*. Archaeological evidence shows significant diplomatic correspondence exchanged between Akhenaton and at least two Kassite Kings: Kadashman Kharloe I and Burnaburiash II. Scholars refer to these clay tablets as the "Amarna Letters"—all of which are written in *cuneiform* and not *Egyptian* characters.

The collection itself is named for the site where they were discovered at in 1887—*Tell el Amarna*—a modern Arabic name for of the ancient city of *Akhenaton*. Cuneiform tablet versions of Mesopotamian epics were also unearthed from there, most likely kept by Egyptian scribes, magician-priests and priestesses for academic purposes.

Toward the end of their rule, the Kassites primary issues were no longer with the Hittites, but instead with a new rising force from the east, *Elam*. These Elamites replaced Mesopotamian dynasties with their own and also succeed in stealing a relic from *Babylon* to their city of *Susa*—the *stele* of the *Code of Khammurabi*. Sovereignty in *Mardukite Babylonia* begins to pass to those *most able*. Salvation of the land often required the "Eye and Hand of Marduk" to pass to foreigners as stewards in wait of launching a *Neo-Babylonian* empire—the "Fourth Dynasty of Babylon."

An *Assyrian* dynastic *patesi*, Marduk-Shapik-Zeri laucnhed campaigns to re-unite the lands in 1200 B.C. This new northern "Assyrian" dynasty included Nabuchadnezzar I ("Nabu-kudurri-usur" in Assyrian) who recovered the *stele* from the Elamites in 1125 B.C. But, real efforts toward a *Neo-Babylonian* empire were quickly thwarted by the Arameans and several small short-lived dynasties. A true "*Babylonian Renaissance*" would have to wait for the proper visionary to manifest.

— 6 —
: RISE OF THE ASSYRIANS :
FROM ASHURBANIPAL TO NEBUCHADNEZZAR II

> *"Even though the Assyrians were 'all powerful' they still had their sense of cultural inferiority – They saw Babylonia as the Source: the best tablets; the 'real' cuneiform culture, much as in the way 19th century Americans might have looked to England as the place where you would find 'real' English literature and such."*
> ~ Jerrold Cooper
> John Hopkins University

Most historians consider the *Assyrians* as simply an extension of ancient Enlilite Sumerians, but they are actually quite more than this. Most of their history and lore, as with the rest of Mesopotamia, has been academically misappropriated. Where the Kassites assisted in carrying over "Mardukite" culture to post-Akkadian Babylonia, the Assyrians were also custodians of the legacy until the greatest heights of "Neo-Babylonian Renaissance," witnessed under the rule of Nebuchadnezzar II, the Chaldeo-Assyrian King of Babylon.

"Assyrian" culture was named for a particular deity—ASSUR or ASHUR. This name applied to the people, the culture and the language, in addition to their native region of the name of their capital city. *Assur, Ashur, Assur, Asar, &tc.*—all of these are derived from an epithet for MARDUK, the god of *Babylon*, and the Assyrians recognized this.

Academic "Assyriologists" ("Sumeriologists," *&tc.*) have often mistakenly attributed the chief Assyrian *Anunnaki god* ASHUR (*"The One Who Sees"*) with the chief deity observed in the original Sumerian pantheon: ENLIL, or at the very least, his heir-son, NINURTA (NINIB). Mardukite records and deductive reasoning rooted in historical consistency would suggest this is not the case. Assyrians observed an Anunnaki tradition centered on MARDUK, but of course in their own language.

The homeland of the *Assyrians*—their kingdom and realm—is more accurately an extension of the *Akkadian* culture—the "Old Babylonians." By 1000 B.C. the *Assyrians* had *Akkadians* populations of *Akkad* and became the next race of ancient-originating Semitic people in Mesopotamia.

As with the Akkadians and Kassites once blessed by MARDUK in times of need, arrival of *Assyrians* in *Babylon* eventually proved positive for its continuing legacy.

A Mardukite emphasis first returns to *Babylonia* with the reign of Nabu-mukin-apli (1000 B.C.) and the eighth dynasty of *Babylon*. This dynasty makes significant cultural efforts toward restoration of Mardukite temples and national statuary—all refinished in gold and *lapis lazuli*, the official "sacred" blue-hued stone of *Babylonia*. This period of peace, prosperity and cultural development began leading the population toward a true *Neo-Babylonian Renaissance*.

But not everything was peaceful in Mesopotamia. Babylonians experienced frequent uprisinging from the western Sutu tribes: nomadic Enlilite Aramaean desert dwellers. Suti even prevented national religio-political festival ceremonies from occurring—on several occasions barring ceremonial procession of the NABU statue from *Borsippa* (a site near *Babylon* sacred to the Babylonian scribe god) during the annual New Year Spring Equinox (A.KI.TI or *Zagmuk*) ceremony. [This national observance involving statuary idols was a symbolic reenactment originating with activities once observed of the Anunnaki themselves when they identifiably walked among the people of earth.]

During this struggle, Nabu-apla-iddina (in *Babylon*) worked to maintain the highest peace with his rivals as possible, including the Assyrian king, Ashurnasipal II. He even formed a peace treaty with Ashurnasipal's son, King Shalmanesar II. Nabu-appla-iddina also launched a "literary" *Renaissance* in *Babylon* (and *Borsippa*) by reviving the "Order of Nabu"—priest-scribes, priestesses and magicians dedicated to salvaging and recopying older cuneiform tablets of esoteric, spiritual (religious), political, astronomical or scientific value.

But, where *Sumerian* tablet-cycles were focused on antiquated establishments of world order, pantheistic hierarchies, divine politics and religion—we see something quite different in post-Sumerian paradigms of the *Assyrians*. The Assyrian paradigm, foregoing religious and spiritual standards, emphasized battle, warfare and militant conquest, particularly what could be credited to a "Legacy of Kings."

Where the previous Mesopotamian Kings were often respected for their role in establishing order by their working *with* the "gods" directly, the Assyrians spend their developmental years focused on territorial disputes and material conquests.

To their credit, however, the Assyrian Empire revolved around the most formidable military force known to the ancient world, introducing standards for many military innovations: cavalry, archery, siege engines, war ships, chariots, and battering rams.

Starting in the Ninth Dynasty of Babylon, King Nabu-nasir (750 B.C.) installed the *"Babylonian Chronicle,"* a practice of event recording for scribe-priests—a kind of "A.N." (*Anno Nabonassan*) dating system used as a local standard during the Nabonassar Era.

Other Kings in the dynasty included Nabu-nadin-zeri (735 B.C.), killed during a riot; and Nabu-suma-ukin II (732 B.C.), replaced after only one month of reign by an Aramaen chief, Nabu-mukin-zeri. He was killed in a siege on *Babylon* by the Assyrians King Tiglath-Pileser III, founder of the Tenth Dynasty of Babylon and the *"Neo-Assyrian Empire."*

In 720 B.C., the throne was assumed by a Chaldean prince, Marduk-apla-iddina II (the biblical *Merodach-Baladan*). He struggled for control of *Babylon* against Sargon II, who succeeded in keeping him out of *Babylon* for over a decade. But after Sargon's death, Marduk-apla-iddina II resumed power of the throne and succeeded in sparking chaotic revolution in *Babylonia* before dying in exile (700 B.C.)—forcing Mesopotamia once again into political confusion for a time.

* * *

Eleven miles southwest of Babylon city, and many years before its modern rediscovery, archaeologist Henry Rawlinson began excavation (in the 1850's) of ruins of a different ancient city—*Borsippa*—the sacred precinct of *Nabu*, the Babylonian god of writing, cuneiform tablets and magic.

At first, archaeologists thought they had discovered the ruins of Babylon, but they had found something else altogether—*Bad-Tibira* in the original Sumerian; or in Babylonian-Akkadian, the name reads *Til-Barsip*. Its present-day Arabic name is *Birs Nimrud*. Among these ancient remains—the E.ZIDA —Nabu's ziggurat *"Temple of the Seven Spheres,"* built on antiquated remains by the first major public Mardukite King—*Hammurabi*—and later restored by the last major Mardukite King—*Nebuchadnezzar II*. [It is from this temple and others in Babylon that the "Seven-fold Order" significant to the "Mardukite Babylonian Anunnaki Tradition" are derived.]

An avid reader and collector of all tablets available in Mesopotamia, the "Royal Library" archives of the Assyrian King, *Ashurbanipal*, maintained a complete record of everything that could be recorded—but in the Assyrian language. This so vastly influenced early archaeologists that scholars named the entire academic field after the collection—"Assyriology." Such intellectual pursuits, however, were not always so prominent among leadership in Mesopotamia as many of the rulers spent most of their time and energies maintaining or expanding their physical realm through battle and conquest.

With the death of *Ashurbanipal* came the fall of Assyrian power in Babylon. The *Babylonians* elected a king from among their own revolutions— *Nabopolassar*. He then joined forces with the *Chaldeans* and the *Medes* in defeating the Assyrians at their capital of *Nineveh*, and then later the *Egyptians*. Aging and war-worn after several successful victories against two empires, he wisely passed power of the throne to his son, while still living. His son—the famous Mardukite King, *Nebuchadnezzar II*.

King Nebuchadnezzar II supported a prosperous pro-*Mardukite* era for nearly fifty years. He maintained peaceful unity of *Sumer* and *Akkad* (*Babylonia*) in the name of *Marduk* and *Nabu*. He restored many city centers and sacred ziggurat temples. Before his death, he predicted an impending end to the glory of his *Chaldean Empire in Babylon* – and the actions of the kings who were to be his successors invariably proved him right. [See also the "Sajaha" Tablet-S Series in "*Necronomicon: The Anunnaki Bible.*"]

The city of Babylon served as a geographic capital of the entire "*Babylonian Empire.*" As a dynamic city-state, the conditions of Babylon constantly adjusted to change in accordance with the forces in play, but one ideal remained constant: the relentless determination to reach an apex of esteem and glory—and according to their tradition, reign by *Divine Right*. Installation of "*Mardukite World Order*" into human consciousness continued to radiate from the city of Babylon; its *Mardukite* designation being, literally —"*Babylon*"—from the Akkadian *bab.ilu*, meaning "*Gateway of the Gods*" or "*Star-Gate to Heaven.*" ["KA.DINGIR.RA.KI." in Sumerian logograms.]

Walking in the shadows of a legacy born from ancient icons—*Sargon* and *Khammurabi*—the third and last legendary "Mardukite King" brought Babylon to unforeseen heights during reign of the *Neo-Babylonian (Chaldean) Dynasty*—*Nebuchadnezzar II*. Following the years of chaotic discord in *Babylonia* and irreverence in the *holy city*, all that had been built or could be restored proper to the national gods—MARDUK and NABU— *Nebuchadnezzar II* commissioned in Babylon during his lifetime.

Before Nabuchadnezzar's death, his heir-son, Awel-Marduk (560 B.C.), also written Amel-Marduk ("Evil Marduk"), reigned for only two years. He usurped the throne against the will of his father (who was still in power) and was murdered by his brother-in-law and successor Nergal-sharezer, in assistance to the true king. None again would be as great as Nabuchadnezzar II. Any short-lived reform efforts to maintain integrity of *Babylonia* were therefore quickly dissolved by one of the most unjust anti-Mardukite Kings of *Babylon* (555 B.C.) in the midst of an otherwise perfect *Mardukite Renaissance*.

Following the death of Nabuchadnezzar II and its chaos, the "Seat of Babylon" was usurped by an Assyrian rebel calling himself *Nabonidus*. His name meant *"Nabu is exalted,"* though his suppression of the Mardukites, desecration of holy sites and violation of countless traditions would indicate that he lived by another creed. *Nabonidus* fell prey to the old Sumerian "cult of the moon god"—the lunar-cult associated with the Anunnaki god NANNA-SIN. *Nabunidus* chose the pre-Babylonian Enlilite "lunar cult" in lieu of following the solar (and stellar traditions) of the Mardukite Babylonians. He even forbid the Mardukite *Akiti* (*Akitu*) "New Year" festival of the spring equinox from taking place. MARDUK was forced to take action, whether literally or in spirit. To prevent the utter annihilation of his people, the "Eye and Hand of Marduk" would again fall upon foreigners.

Cyrus the Great marched on Babylon and rightfully dethroned Nabonidus, igniting the Persian Dynasty of Babylon. His first action upon entering the city—to pray, make sacrifice and participate in nationalist ceremonies at the "Temple of Marduk." In fact, he attributed all of his success in taking control of *Babylon* to the power of the *Anunnaki god* MARDUK. [This is recorded on the Tablet-L Series of *Necronomicon: The Anunnaki Bible*.] His lineage is allowed to continue until the arrival of, and replacement by, the Greek Hellenistic Dynasty of Alexander the Great in 330 B.C.

And the rest, as they say: *Is history...*

— 7 —
: CUNEIFORM TABLETS :
THE BIRTH OF WORLD SYSTEMS

"The education of the Babylonians was entirely in the hands of the priests, who derived their knowledge from Nabu, the inventor of writing and letters, and every kind of learning — the Lord of "Houses of Tablets" (or books), i.e. the first libraries."
~ E.A. Wallis Budge
Babylonian Life & History

The overt observable evolution of Sumerian civilization into a *Babylonian Empire*—the facts—as described previously regarding history, may not altogether seem remarkable on the surface. However, the *seeker* should keep in perspective just how quickly all of this developed from seemingly nothing.

It is true that societal living was originally organized around *state religion*, but prior to this it was culminated not by social relationships shared between people, but by their living relationship with the earth. Where first we have loosely organized nomadic hunter-gatherers forced to wander about or dwell in caves, essentially rolling the dice of chance for their survival, very little time passes before a sweeping urbanization of Mesopotamia, developed around structured agricultural farming and pasturing.

Mesopotamia may be credited with many "*firsts*" during the development of early human history. It is, however, the incorporation and evolution of "writing" that the Sumerians are most esteemed for—something undoubtedly developed by necessity for continuous civic growth, spiritual and scientific progression. In fact, it is *only* with *writing* that we have *any* concept at all of "history." Everything *prior* to this inception for our times, is rightfully considered "prehistoric"—those times accompanied by no written records.

According to ancient cuneiform tablets, the original decision to cultivate civilization in Mesopotamia was not born from men, but from a distinct group of beings known as the *Anunnaki*—those that appeared to "come down from the sky" and were later considered *deities* and *gods* of the original "pantheon"—those who "decree the fate on Earth." Cuneiform tablets also describe Anunnaki motives for "genetically upgrading" humanoids: to make them fit as material workers for these "*gods*."

Prehistoric lore is interpreted from the "Creation & Disposal of Men" cuneiform tablets—Mardukite *Tablet-G* Series in *"Necronomicon: The Anunnaki Bible"*—describing long before what we call the *"Deluge,"* under the direction of these "divine" *overseers*—not yet the mortal priest-kings found in popular historical chronicles—prior to what we know as *"human* civilization."

Anunnaki control of the "heavens" and "aero-space" rested with the god ANU and his son ENLIL, respectively. The material world, however—the realm most integrated with human life—became the domain of ANU's other son, E.A., called ENKI—whose name means "Lord (*En*) of the Earth (*Ki*)" in Babylon. While the majority of ancient Mesopotamia was classified "Enlilite" territory, origins for the esoteric "Arts of Civilization" emerge from ENKI's own southern city of *Eridu* on the ancient coasts of the Persian Gulf. Here we find systematic origins of "true" human civilization. Born of innate necessity and survival of material systems, use of esoteric *"Secret Doctrines"* allowed data to condition the human psyche through integration of "worldly systems." The means by which this has always been executed on earth: "*media*"—the *written word*.

It is evident that practically all ancient cultural "mythologies" share a unique anthropological belief: that indigenous humans were somehow "engineered" apart from their natural evolving timeline on the planet, and further given a knowledge of something "outside of themselves" that was directly responsible for this. *Cuneiform tablets* speak of this "outside" and "intervening" force as a group of beings called *Anunnaki*—though they are known by a myriad of other names as well, particularly among diverse cultures and languages around the globe.

According to the *cuneiform* texts, the *Anunnaki* sought to prepare the earth for habitation, but found the physical nature of the work on earth was not suited to them. They employed their "army"—known as the IGIGI ("Watchers")—to do the manual labor. And after some years pass, even this group revolts. The *Anunnaki* hesitantly decide to upgrade existing hominids, fashioning a new class of "worker." Today, we now see a cliché concept emerging in the "New Age" that acknowledges humans as a slave-species built by and for the "gods"—or at least these "Anunnaki" figureheads later interpreted as the mythological "gods" of antiquity.

The *Sumerians* and *Babylonians* weren't "stupid." The "mythologies" reflected in their writing are not drawn from ignorance or people unaware of "natural phenomenon." Skeptical scholars minimize the true significance of history by putting forth fallacies.

Cuneiform literature left behind suggests a highly intellectual and spiritual culture with a deep understanding of the *cosmos* from the beginning, even when expressed though a limited vocabulary.

Much like early Egyptians using hieroglyphics, the first Sumerian "cuneiform" writing (named in Classical times from the Latin "*cuneus*," meaning "wedge") was also a tradition of picture-writing etched with sticks and fingernails. Refinement of the writing style continued throughout the *Sumerian* age, but around 2100 B.C., the script-form changed dramatically with a gift from NABU for his Babylonian scribe-priests—the reed *stylus* pen. There are many who seem easily dismissive of the current subject matter in this book, or that simply find the topic of *cuneiform tablets* to be boring and without relevance. As a monumental cornerstone in human development, the perfection of writing in Babylon is the very reason we have such vast collections available today to glean lore of this extraordinary and forgotten empire. Without this specific esoteric literary tradition, we would be left clueless.

* * *

Early picture-writing proved sufficient for many things. The goals of its use were simple—primarily survival. Hunting grounds, natural dangers and even some elaborate stories could all be marked with a primitive pictorial language. Humans navigated obstacles of communication easily enough using speech and gesture—so, what then was the purpose of writing?—of the *words that stay?*

All of the civic systems on the planet, those that distinguish the "elevated" social network of the "human animal," depend on a communication relay of the written word to be effective. And with the creation of the stylus, this was accessibly possible—a methodology for "systems" was broadcast wide among the masses. Its successful implementation aided Anunnaki "control" of an exponentially growing human population. But it was a "Mardukite" inception—the result of two efforts: the birth of systems in *Eridu* by ENKI (with the aid of, not surprisingly, his heir-son MARDUK), and also the ratification of writing in *Babylon* by NABU (heir-son of MARDUK) much later. By combining these two facets, the "Arts of Civilization" were activated in Babylonia.

The human psyche became conditioned to societal living, now connecting two aspects internally: *pictures* and *words*. The two were already one in form —as picture writing—but only in the vaguest sense.

Use of a *stylus* changed this by not only speeding up the flow and form of written images, but as a straight-edged tool, this pen eliminated *curvature* of any characters. No longer would someone have need to draw out an image of several animals to depict them. A series of quick hashed-wedge marks could be used to represent it instead—and in the conditioned human consciousness, the two would become inseparable in meaning.

Solidification of abstract concepts and ideas represented as "words" actually changes the way the brain thinks—changes the way in which one experiences these aspects of reality and what the words actually represent. Mentally adopting a label system for fixed nouns and names creates an internal database called a 'schema' which manipulates experiences and affects memory. An academic consensus is that these "perceptions" are evolutionary advantages, adapting one to the environment that an individual is reared to. This certainly was not evolutionarily necessary for the survival of the species, but for the survival of the *system*, by which matters of commerce and state, laws and government, roles and order, religion and trade could all be *fixed* to writing, securing an imprinted history and fate on the human consciousness to *words that stay*.

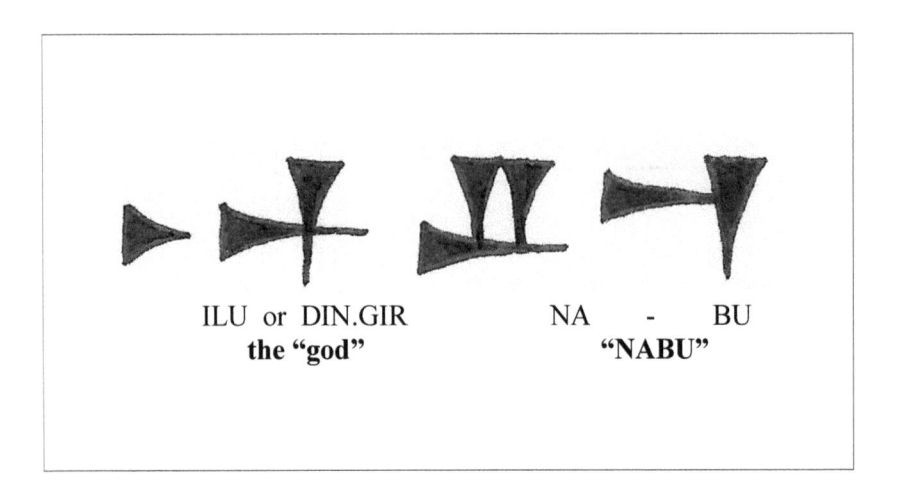

ILU or DIN.GIR
the "god"

NA - BU
"NABU"

The cuneiform wedge-writing system is designed quite differently than more recently used classical alphabets, such as the "Roman" letters this book is printed in. In fact, cuneiform is not an alphabet at all, but a series of symbols used to represent phonetic sounds or "syllables"—typically combinations of a consonant and a vowel. Thus, we have no ancient cuneiform form of a letter "*B*," but there are signs for the sounds: *ab*, *ib*, *ub*, *ba*, *be*, *bi* and *bu*.

Babylonian refined *stylus*-based cuneiform, combined with the ease of clay tablet construction, resulted in a plethora of written records in the ancient world. Eventually, a "royal library" was established in *Babylonia* (often in *Borsippa*) as a Temple of NABU, maintained by the official librarian-priest sometimes known as a *Rab Girginakki* in Akkadian language. Efforts to create and preserve similar "archival libraries" later occurred throughout Mesopotamia—always under the direction of the current *authority* in power. By 2000 B.C., Babylonian law required all transactions be documented and duplicated by official *scribe-priests*.

While writing itself was prevalent, for an exceptionally long period of human history, only higher classes of citizen were required to learn reading and writing. Dependency on scribe-priests as "interpreters of writing" among the common masses became great. Any discovered indiscretion or falsehoods relayed in this process were severely punished, which strengthened the faith of the people in these "life-depending" (and "life defining") public records and deeds of ownership.

By necessity, the *cylinder-seal* was developed—a clay signature-seal uniquely fashioned for an individual and often worn or carried like a large bead long before signet rings. This small cylinder could be *rolled* across a tablet surface to create a rectangular stamp-mark. And just to be sure there was no tampering, the NABU scribe-priests developed a unique way of enclosing and preserving signed clay tablets within clay envelopes with a duplicate signed inscription on the outside. In special circumstances an additional copy would be retained by the archivist. These practices promoted the original form of banking and commerce—trading in kind, complete with a notarized receipt. If this were not enough, a new *system* of conceptual civic wealth was integrated: the possession of land property—or *real estate*— authorized and governed by the state, ownership of which was not represented by physical occupancy, but by *written deeds*.

The full implications of these *Anunnaki, Babylonian,* and *"Mardukite"* systems are not so obvious to the common man—and certainly not to early "Assyriologists" either. Seldom do we consider the covert governing body that originally dictated these systems and regulated their integration into social consciousness. Such might be easily overlooked or taken for granted by contemporary minds thinking of little than one-foot-in-front-of-the-other. And yet it is entirely connected to where humans are, were and will be. Definitions, semantics, knowledge boundaries and the ability to coherently and permanently record them into histories, calendars, maps, property deeds and even "secret esoteric knowledge"— completely and utterly changed human reality experience... *forever!*

— 8 —
: PRIEST-SCRIBES OF NABU :
THE SECRET SOCIETY OF BABYLON

> *"The Palace of Ashurbanipal, King of the World, King of Assyria, who in Assur and Belit puts his trust, on whom Nabu and Tasmitu have bestowed broad ears, who has acquired clear eyes. The valued products of the scribe's art, such as no one among the kings who has gone before me had acquired, the wisdom of Nabu, unequaled, as so much as can be found, I have had inscribed on tablets and arranged in groups. I have revised, and for the sign of my reading, have set in my Palace this library – I, the ruler, who knows the Light of Assur, the King of the Gods."*
> ~ King Ashurbanipal
> *Dedication on the Royal Library*

What academic scholars term *"Babylonian Mythology"* is actually an evolution of the former *Sumerian Anunnaki* legacy—the progression of an archetypal *Anunnaki* family in Mesopotamia and *not* simply a cultural assimilation or reapplication of a similar pantheon. This is what we see in later classical mythoi, such as the Greeks and Romans, which simply regurgitate the same ancient themes with new names. Likewise, the esoteric Babylonian religious and political pantheon should be viewed as an extension of the older Sumerian one. This gives rise to many misunderstandings and misconceptions when interpreting of tablets from varying origins and time periods. In this case, however, the Babylonian spiritual, religious, cultural and political focus is transferred to activities of a "younger generation" of *Anunnaki gods*, as "sealed" coherently in the Babylonian Tradition.

In the "Mardukite" Babylonian paradigm, ANU's position as "heavenly father" (turned "grandfather" by the "younger generation") remains unchallenged, and retains the numeric designation of 60, the perfect *whole* number (like our 100) in Mesopotamian mathematics. Controlling more worldly concerns—the position of "earthly father" for the local universe (numerically designated 50), is a title first bestowed to ENLIL, royal heir of ANU according to "Enlilite" Sumerian tradition. ENLIL's heir-son—NINURTA or NINIB—was next in succession to continue the "Enlilite" legacy. Although ENKI was given the role of "Lord of the Earth" (with a numeric designation of 40), the division between the domains of ENLIL and ENKI blur—both literally and figuratively.

In the Sumerian paradigm ENLIL and ENKI aid one another in the foundation of the material world, but by the time of the Babylonians, each had their own dedicated following—essentially splitting the global population into dualism. According to early Babylonian tablets, this schism first occurred concerning the genetic upgrade of original humans themselves, and then over their "disposal" during the *Deluge*. ENLIL, an *Anunnaki* nationalist, high commander and heir to ANU, was understandably reserved about the creation and assistance of humans. ENKI, the chief scientist and esoteric magician of the *Anunnaki* (with a dynastic line that is not granted the same royal distinction as ENLIL), sees potential in the human race to preserve his own legacy on earth and that of his son, MARDUK.

As cuneiform writing evolved, the face of the religion changed and crystallized into more familiar versions of the Mesopotamian mysteries it is defined by today. Mystical and religious tablets were avidly created in Babylon to not only solidify and protect the traditions, but actually *manipulate* them. This primitive logic is a basis for many semantic *systems* still active today. In short—reality is based on the experience of the *realm*, the world of light that we see and acknowledge stimuli from. The world of light is separated into *forms*, which require *classification* as "things." These *classifications* must work together within a coherent *system* to carry any conceptual or functional meaning. [This is what enables the current author to write these *words* and have a reader comprehend them *later*.]

While basis of writing is to collect "data," it is the interpretation within consciousness that equates it to *facts*. "*Words that stay*" are "*facts*" collected about *reality*—the internal processing of cohesive *experience*. In ancient Mesopotamia, we find historical tablets detailing deeds of kings and cosmological tablets describing the deeds of gods—these are the *beliefs* about *reality* dictated for the population and presented as *facts*. Conclusively, as far as the human condition is concerned: the *written word dictates reality*. And to be fair, while men and kings go to their graves each believing in their own truth, these thousands of years later, it is the *written word* from their era that has survived them all.

* * *

Mardukite priests and priestesses of Babylon were, by nature, *Priests of* ENKI, following a tradition from the ancient *systems* born in *Eridu*. Beyond simply *collecting data* to support a public belief system, the first pragmatic mystical and religious use of writing was the recording of ("esoteric") *Secret Doctrines* and ("exoteric") *incantations*—used later religiously as *appeals* to the *gods* for material worldly assistance.

This developed more *"figuratively"* in time as the temple-shrine *ziggurat*-homes of the *Anunnaki gods* themselves became occupied instead by worldly representatives of the same roles.

In the beginning, people were instructed to petition their needs to the temple-priests and priestesses, who would in turn make appropriate offerings and incantations to the deity involved. This *system* is still installed in society today—in both religion and politics—where ministers or authorities act as intermediaries between citizens and perceptibly "higher powers." Here we see a distinction between the exoteric "surface" *system*-religion of public opinion separate from esoteric practices and traditions of the scribe-priests, temple-priestesses and priest-kings themselves. The *scribes* research and write the tablets, the *temple-priests* enact the tablets and the *kings* enforce the tablets.

Mardukite Babylon could hardly be considered ruled by MARDUK's own lineage—but all of *Babylonia* was still maintained under his care by way of "chosen" priest-kings who were nearly all under the influence of a prestigious secret society—one that changed the shape of Mesopotamia, and the remaining world thereafter, with nearly two millennium of unbroken covert operation in *Babylonia*: the *Priest-Scribes of* NABU.

An unusually enigmatic figure in Mesopotamian history, NABU is listed only among the Babylonian "Mardukite" hierarchy of *Anunnaki gods*. His numeric designation is 12—indicative of cycles, time and esoteric knowledge or "magic." NABU is heir-son to the dynasty of MARDUK, born of SARPANIT, an earth-born wife taken by MARDUK. She was "human," but descended directly from *Adapa*, the first genetically upgraded human by the *Anunnaki god* ENKI (known in Egypt as PTAH). This makes NABU earth-born and little more than half-divine.

NABU shared the dynasty of MARDUK (the Egyptian RA, AMON and ATEN) with an estranged brother, named SUTU (also *Satu* or *Sati*, the Egyptian SETH), whose name means *mountain* or *life of the mountain*. Another "half-brother rival" is listed as ASAR (the Egyptian OSIRIS). Clearly this dynastic family also appears in Egypt under many names, but our current focus is *"Mardukite Babylon."* The name 'NABU' (*"who speaks for"*) indicates a "herald" or "announcer." The word made its way into the Semitic-Hebrew language as *nabih*, meaning "prophet." By the time of "Old" *Mardukite Babylon*—around 2150 B.C., corresponding with the "Age of Aries," the end of the *Old Kingdom* in Egypt and the launch of the "royal" *Dragon Court* by Ankhfn-khonsu—the temple-city and cult center of NABU was localized near *Babylon* at *Borsippa*.

In Babylon, earthborn NABU is transferred the epithet TUTU, replacing a previous Sumerian agricultural goddess—NISABA—who is briefly given credit for pictorial *cuneiform* in Sumerian tradition. As NABU-TUTU he reflects a *"druidic"* role—the Babylonian "nature-deity" called upon at the New Year Festival of *Akiti* to bless the crops and provide fertile land. By that same paradigm, MARDUK would be a "sky-deity," representing a domain of the starry sun that shines down on the land.

In this ancient literary tradition, NABU represents the epitome of the *"pen is mightier than the sword."* Where previous *Anunnaki gods* had cultivated civilization with their contributions—the *cattle and grain* had already been brought, the *pickax* had already been given, *&tc.*—NABU offers the *reed stylus* and reformation of cuneiform writing. This sparked renewed interest in the arts of *Eridu*—the *Secret Doctrines* of esoteric "magic" and science from ENKI and MARDUK. Writing allowed the *"Arts of Civilization"* to be systematized on records of an *Ancient Mystery School*, and NABU is the original guardian of these *"Tablets of Destiny"*—powerful "information" that "sealed" material creation to the *Divine Right* of the *Anunnaki*.

As the "Keeper of Secrets," NABU proved necessary in developing the literary tradition that allowed *Babylon* and the supremacy of MARDUK to be possible. NABU was a mastermind in the company of the most intelligent beings in this corner of the Universe. In the establishment of *Babylon*, NABU was successful in developing his own unique cult following that was often rivaling that of even MARDUK. This original "cult" of NABU still exists even to this day as an esoteric sect called the "Mardukite Chamberlains."

The magic and mysticism of *Babylonia*—born in *Eridu*, then extrapolated and reformed by Mardukite priests, priestesses, magicians and the Order of NABU—was restricted to the priests and treated wholly religious in nature, but rooted in the ancient power and technologies of the *gods*. "Magical" texts from this age are primarily hymns and prayers. The later doctrines or scriptures made public, first originated as historical documents among Mesopotamians, cuneiform tablets chronicling creation and universal order, the genesis of man, the flood cycle and the eventual restoration of civilization. These were all later reinterpreted by other cultures as their own.

Responsibility for forging and preserving this Babylonian literary tradition on clay tablets rested with the Order of Nabu, a secret force that sought to shape the history and future legacy of Babylon in dedication to MARDUK.

Seeing the popularity of the mystical traditions of ENKI to this present day, the familiarity with the "Marduk-versus-Tiamat" Typhonian archetype, the rising interest in the Babylonian systems and Anunnaki in addition to the Freemason and Illuminati attentions originating with this sect—it is the current author's opinion that the efforts of the ancient Order of Nabu proved quite successful.

— 9 —
: MARDUKITE MONOLATRY :
THE STAR-RELIGION OF BABYLON & EGYPT

> *"Marduk's rise to supremacy did not end polytheism— the religious belief in many gods. On the contrary, his supremacy required continued polytheism, for to be supreme to other gods, the existence of other gods was necessary. He was satisfied to let them be, as long as their prerogatives were subject to his control; but what Marduk expected was that they come and stay with him in his envisaged Babylon—prisoners in golden cages, one may say."*
> ~ Zecharia Sitchin
> *Earth Chronicles: End of Days*

The Babylonian *"Star Religion"* of MARDUK sought to "occult" and conceal the previously laden Sumerian religious designations of the *Elder Gods*. Early Sumerian traditions were not very systematic, or even a true "religion," making them easily overlapped by the first clearly defined *systemology*—one that served as an archetype for all later human civilization on the planet. Directly exported forms of this stellar cult included Hermetic Tradition, Atenism, Zoroastrianism, Mithraism, and of course the Semitic-Judeo system.

Original systems integrated into human consciousness were not at first the "monotheism" defined by academic scholars. This appeared later when *Enlilite* standards transformed into *Jehovah* or the Christian "God" as a single personification. In Hebrew, *El* (ENLIL) and *Ia-Yahweh* (ENKI) are separate beings, a belief debated the early Christian Yahwist and Elohist sects. Later Christian authorities likened the ancient myths to "One God" surrounded by *"lesser angels,"* but this still does not adequately explain the anthropomorphic manifestation of the One God on earth being the same as, one-to-one, The Absolute All-present All-knowing All-powerful "Divine Source." We mainly see remnants of this distinction in Gnostic Mysticism, Elohist Christianity and modern Mardukite interpretations.

Contemporary historians often simplify, likening the Mardukite stellar-cult to a religious "monotheistic" standard. But the tradition is more correctly termed: *monolatrism*. This was a confusing concept for some—and probably remains so today—as even the Assyrians were completely *pantheistic*, exalting *Assur* (MARDUK), but venerating and working with many other "personal deities" as representations of the "Divine."

Babylon became the "seat of the gods," but by Mardukite standards, this was intended differently than either *monotheism* or *polytheism* can provide. The basic program became as follows: There are many *gods* but the way is through *One*, idealized in Babylonian tradition as MARDUK and his consort SARPANIT via the holy receptionists, NABU ("Divine Secretary" or "Librarian of Babylon") and his consort TESHMET (or TASMIT), the "Listener of Prayers."

The work performed to usurp the ancient *Fifty Names* from the *Enuma Elis* (*"Epic of Creation"*) for MARDUK also illuminates the idea of "many *gods* as *One*" or the "*One* manifest with many *faces*," but with the central figure on earth always returning to MARDUK as *divine representative*. Assuming the *Fifty Names* connected to an ancient "Divine Decree" of FIFTY—by Anunnaki numeric designation of World Order, equaling the rank of ENLIL, the "Lord of Command."

Babylonian myth and magic systems are dedicated to MARDUK's "Divine World Order." It is illustrated through the original mystical "kabbalah" system: *ten gates, two doors* and *seven levels*—just like the design for MARDUK's *ziggurat*—E.TEMEN.AN.KI—*"The Temple of Heaven and Earth."* These *Ziggurats*—artificial "mountain-home temple-shrines of the gods"—stood as giant stepped-pyramids in honor of the patron deity of a city-state, so named from the *Akkadian* word for them: *"Zi-kur-ra-tu."* And each ancient Mesopotamian city had one.

Of course, stepped pyramids are not only found in Mesopotamia—but many other prehistoric cultures, too. They are unique in function as "residences," seldom seen in more traditional Egyptian pyramids. However the oldest pyramids of Egypt are actually stepped-pyramids. But in Mesopotamia, extraordinarily large stepped pyramids elevated the actual temples, shrines and astronomical observatories—yet they once served as earthly homes for the star-raced "gods" to the most ancient religion on the planet.

Systemology of the "Mardukite" Babylonian Religion reflects many aspects of *animism* and *pantheism*—the belief that everything possesses an innate or inherent "spirit" or *Divine Spark* that entangles it to the "eternity of the cosmos" or *All-as-One*. This "everything" includes fragmentation of distinct personalities or "Self." Cuneiform tablets distinguish these aspects as *utukku* (*Divine Spark* or animating "spiritual essence") and *edimmu* (the "identity program" or soul of the body). In the related Egyptian tradition, these aspects are equated to the *ka* (life-force) and *ba* (personality) of an individual being.

THE EVOLUTION OF RELIGIO-MAGICAL SYSTEMS

Sumerian	*Unity, celestial-cosmic*
Babylonian	*Hierarchy, temple-religions*
Egyptian/Hermetic	*Names, magical-mysticism*
Sumerian	*Petition to the Most High*
Babylonian	*Petition to a pantheon*
Egyptian/Hermetic	*Petition to hierarchy of spirits*

NABU-scribes forged the *Enuma Elis*—a kind of cosmogenetic "*Epic of Creation*" central to the religion. But, the political purpose of this document was to bestow MARDUK with the "*Tablets of Destiny*," enabling him world control or World Order. The covert cosmological beliefs were, however, actually *monistic*. This means that the *Divine Source* represents a single unifying principle, agent or "element" (referred to in some materials as the *All-as-One*) defining: One Existence - One Truth – One Cosmic Law. The later philosophy and practices of *Hermetic mysticism* are, therefore, not "invented" during the classical age, but are actually imported from a more antiquated *Ancient Mystery School* born in Babylon.

— 10 —
: MARDUK & THE ANUNNAKI :
MESOPOTAMIAN MYTHOLOGY IN BABYLON

> *"Like Napolean, who decided he did not need to be crowned according to the rules and crowned himself without further ado, so the Assyrian priests gave the honor to Ashur simply by taking the old Babylonian tablets and recopying them, substituting the name of their own god for that of Marduk. The work was not very carefully done, and in some places the name of Marduk still creeps in. . ."*
> ~ Edward Chiera
> *They Wrote on Clay*

Babylonian literary tradition, in addition to implementing a social system, focused primarily on one thing: *religious myths*. The Mesopotamian "mythos" is not called such to indicate any *fictions*. The real meaning of a *mythos* or *mythoi* in human history concerns the *systemology* of human consciousness —a paradigm of reality. Thus, a "mythology" was once little more than documentation of history—the deeds of gods, demigods and kings. Cultural emphasis on these characters is what, in essence, *creates* a mythology—a way of seeing the world as shared by a large group. It didn't take long for this methodology to be *covertly manipulated* to serve the political integrity of the *Babylonian Empire*.

Historically, "mythology" emphasizes activities that few relate to today—human interaction with the *"gods."* More often than not, descriptions of these encounters commonly involve a particular geographic feature—*mountains*. And where mountains were not accessible, the *gods* worked in conjunction with *humans* to construct *"zikkurat"-pyramids*, from the Akkadian description *"zaqaru"*—"artificially built mounds." In Sumerian language, the word for mountain is *kur*, the same as their name for the "primordial dragon" of the cosmos in pre-Babylonian mythology.

Surviving cuneiform tablet-sources intermittently make mention of *"dragons."* At some juncture; the "universe," the "planet earth" and the "blood of men" are all coined "dragon" in nature. The first legendary figures confronting "dragons" become *archetypes* for the "King of the Mountain." In the oldest Sumerian versions, these are ENLIL, NINURTA and even INANNA-ISHTAR. Given that "Enlilite" patina on these records, the name of MARDUK appears nowhere on these original epic tablet-cycles.

During the early Sumerian age, MARDUK—called ASARLULI—was the first "magician-priest" of *Eridu*. This cult center from antediluvian times was later known in legend to the Greeks in their own language and mythic interpretation as the "*Temple of Poseidon*." Therefore, although there are many "lost civilizations" on the planet, scholars have confused semantics regarding the Greek renderings of "*Atlantis*"—information they recovered from the Egyptians long after the fact.

The Babylonian "*Epic of Creation*" (academically named "*Enuma Elis*" for its opening lines) was often observed in ancient traditions for its "*systemological*" value above its "*cosmogenetic*" qualities. However, it is *set* in a time before "earth" or "men" and describes the evolution of them both out of an unfolding "created universe"—progressive "*fragmentation*" of the *All-as-One* into parts. This has esoteric implications quite unique to ancient "Mardukite" lore—As already fragmented being the "*Anunna*" the "Secret Doctrines of the Cosmos," as used them to their advantage systematically when dealing with "humans."

In the "*Enuma Elis*" we are given a political account of MARDUK slaying the "cosmic serpent" or *dragon*, representing his "overcoming of chaos" in the cosmos to establish his own universal or "world order." This was actually an "old concept" revived from pre-Babylonian (Sumerian) use of the *kur* in earlier mythologies. By performing this feat or conquest, MARDUK became the "*King of the Anunnaki*," a title was bestowed upon him (according to the "*Enuma Elis*") as a reward from the "*Council of Anunnaki*" for his dragon-slaying feat. Performing this feat, even if only symbolically and in archetypal consciousness, the "Mardukite" forces are given *Divine Right* to exercise the powers of the *Anunnaki* on Earth.

The *Enuma Elis* forms the cornerstone of Mardukite usurpation of the Sumerian Anunnaki hierarchy. The work also illustrates a distinction between eras of older generations: a race of "*Ancient Ones*" led by the primordial dragon, TIAMAT; the "Elder Gods" or *Anunna* of prehistorical renown, such as ANU, ENLIL and ENKI; and a "Younger Generation" of *Anunnaki* in the Babylonian pantheon under MARDUK, which included many of his Enlilite peers: NANNA-SIN, INANNA-ISHTAR, SAMAS (SHAMMASH) and NERGAL.

While in *Eridu*, MARDUK is not actually attributed among early Sumerian *Anunnaki gods*—not listed among the pantheon. In fact, MARDUK is initially the primary high-ranked leader of the IGIGI ("Watchers") and during this role sets a new *status quo* in *Eridu*—and then in *Babylon*—concerning intermarriage between *Anunnaki* with humans.

For this "indiscretion," by Enlilite "World Order" standards, he was denied any future *Divine Right*. His argument remained that he was never going to be given his *"Right"* anyway, and furthermore, that his chosen consort, SARPANIT, was a seventh generation descendent of *Adapa*, the hybrid man born from direct genetics of ENKI, and therefore "Dragonblood." But the decree had been made. If it would not be *given* in order to reign on Earth in Babylon during his time—the *Age of Aries*—then "Divine Right" would have to be *taken*.

* * *

Contemporary archaeologists first became aware of the Babylonian *"Epic of Creation"* cycle in 1849, when cuneiform tablets were recovered during an expedition of the "Royal Library of Ashurbanipal" in *Nineveh*. Its contents were first published academically in 1876. They received significant attention from historians, mythographers and biblical scholars—not only because of their antiquity, but because of how significant the work turned out to be in deciphering the "methodology" of all ancient religions. In short—scholars discovered that the Babylonian *"Epic of Creation"* was the basis of the Judeo-Christian *"Book of Genesis."* But, after so many centuries of misinformation, *who would believe it?*

Multiple versions of the *"Enuma Elis"* and other Mesopotamian creation-cycles exist but there is one key element that many esoteric practitioners and academic historians miss when appropriating origins for the tablets within the "bigger picture." All tablet-cycles making reference to "MARDUK" at all, are purely *Babylonian*—not Sumerian. They reflect usurpation and transfer of "power" in Mesopotamia to *Babylon*, the control of the empire by priest-magicians, priestesses and dragon-kings—authorities of religious and spiritual systems for the people and their relationship with the "Gods." The usurpation was covert. Publicly, "Divine Right" *could* be demonstrated to coincide with the "World Order" decreed by ANU, ENLIL and ENKI in prehistoric times, *using* the *Enuma Elis* to elevate MARDUK and develop *Babylon* as the earthly seat of godly power!

ENUMA-ELIS : THE SEVEN TABLETS OF CREATION

I.
a.)—ABSU (*the Abyss*) and TIAMAT (*the Cosmic Dragon*) are first forms form the One (*All*).
b.)—Generations of "gods" are born and begin to make too much noise.

c.)—TIAMAT entrusts her vizier KINGU the power to fight for her.
d.)—TIAMAT creates calamity and a horde of monsters as ammunition.

II.
a.)—ENKI reveals the plot against the gods to ANSAR.
b.)—A primary discourse from the first tablet is repeated.

III.
a.)—ANU, ENLIL and ENKI do not stand fit to battle against TIAMAT.
b.)—MARDUK is petitioned to champion the Anunnaki gods.
c.)—MARDUK asks for supreme divinity if successful; to be the *Chief God*.

IV.
a.)—The Anunnaki agree to MARDUK's terms and prepare him for battle.
b.)—MARDUK receives a "cloak of invisibility."
c.)—MARDUK enchants his favored weapon: a bow.
d.)—MARDUK destroys KINGU with a thunderbolt.
e.)—TIAMAT is slain; her minions are scattered and sent to "secret places."
f.)—MARDUK fashions a "*Gate*" to seal these energies separate from the material universe.

V.
a.)—MARDUK seals the cosmic systems of "Lights," "Spheres" and "Degrees" under himself.
b.)—The material-matix *below* is fragmented by the "seven," while the *heights* remain divided into "twelve."
c.)—The "*Anunnaki Star-Gate*" system is sealed throughout the Universe.
d.)—MARDUK sets up a throne for himself next to ANU.

VI.
a.)—The Anunnaki praise MARDUK for his feats.
b.)—The "Key to the Gate" (of the *Abyss* and the *Dragon*) is "hidden" in genetic memory of the "*Race of Marduk*," including humans upgraded by ENKI.
c.)—Babylonian systematization begins.

VII.
    a.)—Having slayed TIAMAT and granted power over material creation, MARDUK takes the names and numbers of ENLIL.
    b.)—MARDUK takes the "signs" and esoteric knowledge ("magic") of ENKI.
    c.)—MARDUK fractures then seals all systems on Earth under his name.

Politically, the *Enuma Elis* allowed the *"Law of Marduk"* (for example, the *"Code of Hammurabi"*) to be upheld. In religious ceremonies—such as the Babylonian New Year Akiti Festival—the *Enuma Elis* was part of the preliminary "rites" conducted of any public or private working. Any significant rituals and even smaller operations of "magic" or "personal devotion" (within the tradition) were usually "opened" with a recitation of the *Epic*. The words cement the basis of all *Mardukite "magic"*—a term used by anthropologists and esoteric practitioners of the Mardukite movement, but which the ancients simply viewed as *"Life."*

The older public ("exoteric") Sumerian *Epics of Creation* are hardly true creation "epics." Their systematic or quasi-cosmological basis is often restricted to a few opening lines, such as:

> *AN carries off heaven;*
> *ENLIL carries off earth.*

To a purely pre-Babylonian *"Sumerian"* cosmology, this simplistic methodology simply *stood* by its own right unquestioned. Such simply *was* and had *always been*. To glean anything deeper, one would have had to become initiated to the "mystery tradition" observed by Babylonian magicians and scribes—the overseers of the "Realm" that supported the *"Dragon-Kings"* ruling by the "Divine Right" of their *"dragon blood"* that originally "descended from the heavens"—from the "gods."

A more physical representation of the *"dragon"* also appears in *Babylon*, though surviving records are obscure. MARDUK had two half-brothers (fathered by ENKI but not necessarily born of NINKI)—NINGISZIDA (*Ningishzidda* or *Ni-(n)rah*) and NINAZU or *Tis(h)pak*. The famous "Dragon of Babylon" first belonged to TISPAK, was later given to MARDUK (as shown in popular artistic depictions) and eventually it came to to the care of NABU. The best renderings are left left Nebuchadnezzar II in his construction of walls and gates of the Babylonian Renaissance.

The traditional name for the dragon name is *Sirius* or *Sirrus,* sometimes spelled phonetically as *"Sirush"* or *"Sirrush."* In Akkadian, the name for the species is *mushussu* or *mushhushshu*, meaning "furious serpent," from *mush-us,* or "monster." [This species should not be confused with the *usumgal*, or "Great Cosmic Serpent" used to represent the universe.] Far away in the African Congo, a description of the *mushussu* matches a species of *sauropod* (now believed to be extinct) called *mokele-mbembe* by the indigenous tribes who claimed to have killed one. This could effectively connect dragon-lore with the (*sa-ru-us/saurus*) dinosaurs. Yet, where dragon-lore is universal, contemporary knowledge of dinosaurs has only been in public evidence for the last 200 years.

"Mastery of Dragons" has long-standing associations with *godhood* ever since these earliest renderings. Evidence still remains in Judeo-Christian lore: the *One God* was eventually seen as 'too great' to be concerned with mortal battle and so the 'dragon-slaying' motif was passed on to "ambassadors" or "emissaries" of God—first *St. Michael* (the archangel most closely associated with MARDUK) and then among chosen mortals like *St. George*. Overt publicly visible possession of a live dragon as both a *royal pet* and *icon* of the holy city further led to securing a worldly "seat of god" for *Babylon* in the consciousness of the masses.

— 11 —
: BABYLONIAN MAGIC :
THE ART OF PRIESTS, MAGICIANS & KINGS

> *"Systematic traditions, 'hermetically sealed' within themselves, later rose from Semitic grimoire-styled ceremonial magic, not surprisingly influenced by 'Egypto-Babylonian' forms of ritual magic—first the domain of Enki and then Marduk and his scribe-son Nabu. Priest-magicians of Babylon would not actually have personally used 'grimoire-like' magic themselves. This was not their way. At best, They invoked the powers of the Anunnaki with incantations in the name of Marduk—but the manner of using 'secret names' as properties of Marduk, or any other demigod, is a much more recent addition to the Hermetic system..."*
> ~ Joshua Free
> –From the original Liber R

Under the banner of a *"New Age movement"* led by *"esotericists,"* we are witnessing a revival of pragmatic spiritual and ritualistic elements drawn from ancient pagan and occult methodologies. We should be seeing no shortage of authentic Mesopotamian lore—being the origin of these later *systems*. But this information is not readily accessible and esoteric success is not achieved via pouring through a *kabbalastic grimoire* written by some *medieval sorcerer*. For this, the *seeker* will have to dig a little harder in the desert sands – into the heart of the true and authentic, antiquated and originating arts of the priests, priestesses, magicians and kings!

During the era of the first *ziggurat* temples—the *Anunnaki* age—all "magic" constituted "spiritual assistance" governed by the state, ruled by priest-kings and temple attendants. All official "mystics" of *Babylonia* were employed by the temples and scribe-houses. There were undoubtedly many others with access to esoteric knowledge who confined themselves to their arts in the *outlands*, beyond the awareness of the societal "realm." The "common" class in Mesopotamia, however, did not really practice "magic" in the way it is generally classified by anthropologists. Personal religious devotions were primarily composed of *hymns* and *prayers* learned from the temples.

Cuneiform tablets describing conduct of "magical" ceremonies list required religious artifacts and items that the average person would not have access to or the ability to afford. *"Magic"* from this period is restricted to the priest class.

Use of a temple, for one, appears key—a tradition continued among some elite modern *lodges* of "ceremonial magic." Access to the tablets themselves—records and *"incantation-prayers"* maintained directly by the priests—was not generally given to just anyone. And you had to be able to read them and memorize them. General collections of these tablets were seldom kept, with the exception of priest-kings maintaining their own personal libraries.

According to *Mardukite Tablet-B*, from *"Necronomicon: The Anunnaki Bible"*—

> *"The priest is always to observe the pious ways, and the Rites of Offering at the Altar of Sacrifice. This is traditional performed by intoning prayers [incantations] from the tablets in conjunction with the offering of incense, grain [bread], honey [with butter] and libations of buttermilk (and in some cases, wine). Sacred or "holy" oil [and water] make an appearance in virtually all ancient Babylonian rites—the water and oil frequently placed in bowls before icons [of deities] in temples, in addition to offerings of alabaster, gold and lapis lazuli."*

At the temple-shrines, the Altar of Offering was set before the *"Boat of the Gods."* The same imagery appears in Egyptian Tradition—a "Boat of the Gods" carrying seven figures, *e.g.* the *Seven Anunnaki Gods* of the Babylonian "Younger Generation." Smaller personal altars could surely be constructed by a devotee appealing to their *god*, but became more prominent with the rise of *"figurative mysticism,"* because originally, these offerings would be physically received by a *god*, or via their "priestly secretaries." Common religious offerings included food and drink, incense and oil, even lavish jewelry and clothing, all of which were carried up the *ziggurat* steps—up the *"ladder to heaven"*—to be placed before the feet of the *god*. When the *gods*, themselves, were not present, it was customary to have an *official* piece of statuary left in their place. Thus, it is easy to see how these original activities evolved into later *magical* and *religious* practices.

White was the most common color worn by the priests, although black was also used and even favored by the temple-priestesses. Priestly attire included the infamous "conical hat," popularly associated today with classical "wizards," but which can be seen worn by *gods*, kings, priestesses and priest-magicans in ancient Mesopotamia, Egypt and eventually elsewhere. Gold and *lapis lazuli* commonly appear as both "magical ritual aids" and prestigious offerings to the gods. Babylonian temples and sacred structures were often designed to radiate these hues.

Wands, necklaces and carried bags of loose *lapis lazuli* are often mentioned on esoteric tablets, in addition to golden rings and "amulet-plates" marked with specific seals and cuneiform glyphs.

Modern implementation of a "practical magical system" based on the "Mardukite" Babylonian paradigm is different than what the contemporary mind —even an *"esoteric"* one—is fundamentally familiar with. As opposed to later magicians who appear to have had to connive and fool hierarchies of spirits into assisting them, threatening them and even in fear of some retroactive revenge, the original magical system used by priests and priestesses of *Babylonia* was rooted in a deep personal relationship of "authority" with the cosmos. Scribes maintained the "sources" of not only their religious power, but a fundamental system of civilization promoting progression of the human species into today. All of this, according to tradition, rested in the power of the *Anunnaki gods*—and the priest-kings and scribes were installed to be sure this was never forgotten.

— 12 —
: STARGATES OF BABYLON :
THE ANUNNAKI POWER OF STARFIRE

> *"True indeed, there was a supreme name which possessed the power of commanding the gods and extracting from them a perfect obedience, but that name remained the inviolable secret of Enki. In exceptional cases the priest besought Enki, through the mediator Marduk, to pronounce the solemn word in order to reestablish order in the world and restrain the powers of the Abyss. But the priest did not know that name, and could not in consequence introduce it into his formulae... He could not obtain or make use of it, he only requested the god who knew it to employ it, without endeavoring to penetrate the terrible secret himself."*
> ~ M. Lenormant
> *Chaldean Magic & Sorcery*

Compared to a more recent world full of "magical" folk traditions—where love potions are in no short supply and acquisition of cosmic favor is as a matter of spinning around seven times while whistling or throwing feathers to the north winds—the original stoic and sacred rites of "divine magic" are rooted in a "mystical" tradition based on a direct relationship, and personal "authority" *earned*, with the *Anunnaki gods*. The mere existence of an ancient "Anunnaki hierarchy" produced the later mystical and religious concept of *"spiritual pantheons"*—pantheons cataloged by *kabbalistic magicians* in later attempts to uncover the "secret of the ages," or more specifically, the secret *"magic word"* that granted authority with the *forces* of the *cosmos*.

In regards to modern "Mardukite" revivals by any practitioner or group—since such cultural revisits are common in the "New Age" mystical paradigms—the *specific* ancient ideology put forth in this book should be kept in mind, particularly if performing "meditations" or metaphysical experiments. Connecting true esoteric knowledge—one-to-one—with physical symbolism or graphic representations, is another important key for effective mystical revival traditions. For example, in the absence of access to the shrines of Babylon and physical *ziggurat* temples, modern practitioners often use "creative visualization," advanced "meditation" techniques, or other mystical methods of "astral travel" to connect with the same "energetic forces."

Contrary to some beliefs, the *Anunnaki* specifically, are not the "UFO-driving aliens" heard of today. However, the *Anunnaki* are very powerful beings who made such deep impressions on the "Akashic Field" that their identities still remain accessible today.

Modern psychology, quantum physics, and practical mysticism all suggest that the energetic self does not properly distinguish a reality barrier between what it encounters or experiences in the body as "day-to-day" from what is possible in properly executed ritual drama. In ancient times, the priests and priestesses reinforced cultural beliefs in society through dramatic reenactments of ancient myths, thereby making them part of "day-to-day" social consciousness—allowing for this "*magic*" to become *reality*. All of it, of course, *really* being a matter of *perspective*. For whatever we may attribute to our "accomplishments of things," it is our belief that we can execute them that makes anything possible.

The Babylonian "Religio-Magic" System was developed by ancient *Mardukites* as a means of sealing power of an older generation of *gods* under MARDUK—with his holding a "*kingship*" over the "younger generation" of *Anunnaki* that served devotional needs of post-Sumerian *Babylonia*. Thus, cosmic power was accessed *through him* and worldly power was dispatched *by him*. And, so long as they could be honored within the confines of the prescribed system, "Enlilite" figures such as INANNA (ISHTAR), NERGAL (ERRA), NANNA (SIN) and SHAMMASH/SAMAS (UTTU) and NINURTA (NINIB) all appear within the younger pantheon observed by the *Mardukites* even though they are *not* descendents of ENKI (as are MARDUK, SARPANIT and NABU). "*Sealing*" this *system* in Babylon is what caused the city-name to be interpreted literally as the "*Gate of the Gods*"— "*bab*" (as "gateway") and "*ilu*" (meaning, "god," "star" or "heaven").

The archetypal theme of "gateways" appears at the heart and soul of all esoteric "religion" and "spirituality" born in Mesopotamia. When we are confronted with matters of the "divine"—or that which is *otherworldly* (of the "*other*")—the symbolism of the "*gate*" is nearly always present. As the mind perceives it, "*gates*" are literally "thresholds," "portals," "doorways" and "windows" into what is deemed *Other*—what is *beyond* our preset daily awareness. The "*Secret Doctrines*" suggest there is only *one* reality—one existence in wholeness—but fragmented (from our point of view) into arbitrary parts via these "veils," "levels," "layers" and other "boundaries" of existence and awareness.

* * *

Since the 1970's practical efforts have been made toward modern revival of a "Mardukite" Babylonian "Gatekeeping" (or "Gatewalking") tradition. But most available lore is derived from ancient literature describing an era of history when priests, priestesses and magicians worked alongside *Anunnaki gods* in establishing and preserving physical *gates* and *shrines*. These structures clearly served multiple purposes in the ancient paradigm, both those that were known to the population—and those unknown.

Following in the pious footsteps of *Babylonian priests*, whether a modern *seeker* or revivalist *practitioner* has been truly *self-honestly* dedicated to the *system* or not, the primordial power of these currents, to be useful or channeled directly—must be first respected. This path, if it is to be applied today, requires cumulatively developed "spiritual authority" developed from working with the archetypal currents of this pantheon with "techniques" dating back to a ancient time of kings, priests, priestesses and magicians.

The "*magic*," then—if we are to call it that—comes directly from a *working* relationship between the individual (priest or magician) and the "powers" controlling the specified domains. In the ancient world, all facets of life were thought to be the domain or under the influence of some "unseen" force—but a force that could be understood and communicated with through magic and religion. This led to the solidification of civilized humans under a "world order"—but one that was transmutable and subject to additional programming and control.

For modern purposes, the term "*Gatekeeping*" or "*Gatewalking*" really applies to the "Mardukite" (*Babylonian*) specific method of *kabbalistic* "pathworking"—predating and serving as origins for the more commonly known Semitic "*Kabbalah*" (or "Cabala"). The methodology is used today by modern "*Mardukite Chamberlains*"—those who actively participate in a revival of the ancient *Mardukite* paradigm as it applies to the modern world. [*Mardukite Chamberlains* are an *active* branch of an otherwise *passive* research organization rooted in both scholarly and esoteric purposes.]

Where a temple is not accessible, "*magic carpets*" and "*statuary*" is set out to consecrate areas for *priestly magic*. Some ritual texts refer to an "*image of your god and goddess,*" and others mention a line of "*seven winged figures*" indicative of the "Younger Generation." As is common in modern traditions, personal sacred space (outside of the temple) is observed as a *mandala* or "sacred circle." Representing ceremony and agriculture, the boundary of the circle was originally marked by consecrated "*flour of Nisaba*"—or the "*flour of Nabu,*" as Babylonian tradition evolved. This is performed the same way a modern "*esotericist*" might draw theirs ritual circle in chalk, *&tc*.

As advice to the priest or magician, the *Tablet-Q Series* in "*Necronomicon: The Anunnaki Bible*" offers this step—

> "*Make your invocation to Marduk and Sarpanit. Then call in [invoke] the Supernal Trinity—Anu, Enlil and Enki, followed by a conjuration [consecration] of the Fire and Four Beacons [lamps] of the Watchtowers [cardinal directions]. Perform the 'Incantation of Eridu' and call forth the presence of your personal sedu [guardian watcher spirit].*"

As a very ancient belief, using mystical conjuration to summon a "personal watcher-spirit" is not unique only to Egypto-Babylonian or *Hermetic* systems. The *sedu* (meaning "spirit," "genius" or "intelligence," much like the Greek word "*daemon*") is also the origins of an Assyrian concept later relayed as the more commonly known "guardian angel" in later Semitic traditions. According to Babylonian beliefs, every person *had* one. This belief may not have been shared by all since lines from some of the original incantations are requests to initially "acquire" a *sedu* and a *lamassu*. In either case, we are again confronted with a "magic" that carries a strength dependent on one's own true understanding and personal relationship with the cosmos.

There are many types of "beings" in the universe, the *Anunnaki* are only one —perhaps the first—to engineer reality for humans on Earth. These "angelic" traditions become more mysterious as they evolved. Identities of IGIGI-"Watcher" spirits fade when contrasted to a host of other forces in existence—some of them seeming *malignant*. During the ancient Mesopotamian age, the "Demonic Spirits" that humans required protection from were often the resonance of pestilence and warfare. Most of the ancient *taboo*-sins or "*bans*" (listed in "*Necronomicon: The Anunnaki Bible*") were meant to keep the people clean and free of infections and disease. Laws were put forth to keep people civil, without them having to murder or eat one another.

A regiment of strict personal cleanliness was essential among the priest and magician class—not only in their conductance of ceremony, but in their everyday walking lives as well. Keeping hair trimmed, or even shaved, was a part of daily ritual—it aided in thwarting personal insect infestations. Use of eye makeup, once thought to be purely decorative, actually had some evolutionary advantages for desert living. Black eye-shadow, particularly beneath the eyes (as used by today's athletes) assists in reducing the sun-glare common to open sandy areas.

"Divine Names" play a key role in both ancient and modern magical or priestly (mystic) work. Sometimes several "names" or mythic "titles" for the same entity are invoked. Even the priest-magician must proposition the *gods* by properly introducing himself with recitation of his lineage. For example, "*I, so-and-so, the son of so-and-so and so-and-so, whose god and goddess is so-and-so and so-and-so. . .*" All of the spoken words involved are really, then, quite direct. *Who are you? Who are you calling? What is the message?* —Just as if you are dealing with a *Divine Secretary*, and yes, the Babylonians even installed NABU and TESHMET to this real position! The system is very "formal."

Keep in mind that the entire effectiveness of the priest's magical work was based on their personal relationship with the *gods*—not simply their ability to discern a *secret number* or precisely memorize an *incantation formula*. These later "magical" beliefs evolved more recently as the *gods* seemed to become more distant from our world.

Original ritualized *petitions* for "divine" assistance seem more akin to requesting help from a *friend* or *authority*. There is a certain measure of *tact* involved, perhaps once common knowledge, that later developed as "occult correspondences." In this case—*This one is only home after 5. That one is more content around the smell of roses. Offer to take this one to lunch first. Mondays are NOT that one's day! &tc. &tc*. How often is this true of our own "Judicial System" even today? Those who made this work their everyday lives in the temples generally knew this type of information, particularly in regards to their own patron deities.

Circulation of "*grimoires,*" "*prayerbooks*" or unauthorized "*spellbooks*" among the masses began as the system evolved from those "outside" the ranks of the national tradition—from those not even sworn to its sanctity. Secrets of the "Ancient Mystery School" are not dependent on widespread dispersion for them to exist—the Power is there for *any* that choose to take it.

— 13 —
: MARDUKITE MAGIC :
ANCIENT RITES & RITUALS OF ERIDU

> *"Through Marduk, the power of Eridu—incantation-prayer and "intention"—was taught to the scribes of Nabu and the Mardukite Priests, who were taught to attract and compel the 'gods' in the name of Marduk, always incanting the word-formula of the highest order: Nabu invoked by way of the name of Marduk; Marduk invoked by way of the name of Enki, Our Father, who in turn would invoke by the name of Anu—and so was born the concept of magical hierarchies, an ideal that was convoluted and obscured when employed later (during the Middle Ages and such), particularly distorted by the Judeo-Christian paradigm as evident in many popular grimoires"*
> ~ Joshua Free
> —Book of Marduk by Nabu
> *Necronomicon: The Anunnaki Bible*

A modern seeker interested in esoteric philosophies has undoubtedly found countless "primers" of magic and sorcery or other ritual "grimoires." Many contemporary guides employ "creative visualization" and "New Thought" techniques—the same ones used by popular self-help gurus and motivational mentors—as well as other forms of meditation, conscious breathing, mental concentration or focus of will. These methods are actually quite effective in the right hands. The material world experienced by an individual is subject to that person's own "energies" and perspective (internal "set") in addition to their interactions with other "energies." Nonetheless, physical "ceremony" is often sought as a necessary step in crossing the thresholds of our own psyche.

Many versions of *"Erudite"* magic are found throughout Mesopotamian "religio-spiritual" (or "magical") cuneiform tablets. Incantations used in the "Mardukite Babylonian Anunnaki Tradition"—from those tablets forged by priest-scribes of the *Order of Nabu*—are actually invoked from the "perspective" (*"authority"*) of NABU. This reflects how the tradition was learned verbatim from MARDUK.

Both scholarly and esoteric texts concur that the "Opening Ritual" for *Mardukite magic* originates with a rite called—*"The Incantation of Eridu."* It is perhaps the most fundamental "formula" of the magical system in *Babylonia*.

It returns one's focus to the heart of the *system* and the roles of its main figures—NABU as "Director," and the appropriation of his father, MARDUK as the "Chief." This is what is acknowledged in the "*Incantation of Eridu*," also known as the "*Incantation of the Deep*," alluding to another name for the far-away abode of ENKI near the *Persian Gulf*.

Ceremonial "affirmations" activate the "*covenant*" of Anunnaki power sealed in *Eridu*, and then in *Babylon*. This allows a practitioner to assume a representative "*god-form*" as the "*Priest of Eridu*"—a title first bestowed upon MARDUK by ENKI in the Sumerian age, then passed onto NABU during standardization of the *Babylonian* era. An esoteric key is in effect here. The priest or priestess conducts the "incantations" ("ceremony") as an embodiment of the intermediary "messenger" *deity*. This is the original meaning of the word "*invocation*." The priest is *not* "evoking" or "conjuring" some apparition—he is directing the flow of *Cosmic Order* by calling specific personality energies "into" *himself*.

The magician is *approaching* his deity as himself—*a servant priest*—and petitions to assume the *godform*, whereby he continues the ceremony as a *divine representation* of the invoked *god*. Similar principles appear within Semitic mysticism and the Judeo-Kabbalah. An an excellent ceremonial example is found in contemporary Catholicism, when the priest "*assumes the Christ-form*" to effectively perform "alchemical transmutation" on the sacramental bread and wine. He conducts this rite as a representative of Jesus on earth, an imitative ritual drama, reenacting the "Last Supper." In the "Mardukite" system observed in *Babylon*, the god invoked is typically MARDUK. This is affirmed with the priest's first utterance of—"*It is not I, but Marduk, who speaks the incantation*"—activating and sealing the system for "practical" use.

Consider the lines of this incantation, adapted for the Mardukite "*Conjuration of the Fire God*" from *Tablet-Y* series in "*Necronomicon: The Anunnaki Bible*"—

> *It is not I, but Marduk, Slayer of Serpents,*
> *Who summons thee.*
> *It is not I, but Enki, Father of the Magicians,*
> *Who calls thee here now.*

As previously introduced, the ritual operates from the perspective ("*authority*") of NABU, speaking for MARDUK. Many variations of this rite exist, including several Assyrian "exorcisms." As an example, one of these cuneiform tablets, translated by R.C. Thompson, relates the opening lines—

> *The Priest of E.A. [Enki] am I.*
> *The priest of Damkina [Ninki] am I.*
> *The messenger [Nabu] of Marduk am I.*
> *My spell is the spell of E.A [Enki].*
> *My incantation is the incantation of Marduk.*
> *The 'magic circle' of EA [Enki] is in my hand.*
> *The 'tamarask' of ANU, in my hand, I hold.*

Opening lines from the modern *Mardukite* version in *Tablet-Y* read—

> *I am the Priest of Marduk,*
> *Son of Our Father, Enki.*
> *I am the Priest of Eridu,*
> *And the Magician of Babylon.*

The Assyrian version continues as follows—

> *EA [Enki], King of the Deep*
> *See me favorably.*
> *I, the magician, am thy slave.*
> *March thou on my right hand,*
> *Assist me on my left;*
> *Add thy pure spell to mine.*
> *Add thy pure voice to mine.*
> *O god that blesses me, Marduk,*
> *Let me be blessed, wherever my path rests.*
> *Thy power, shall god and man proclaim.*
> *And I too, the magician, thy slave.*

E.A. Budge translated an older version for "*Babylonian Life & History,*" where we see another Mardukite method for petitioning the "younger pantheon" of Anunnaki to the side of the priest—

> *I am the Priest of EA [Enki].*
> *I am the Magician of Eridu.*
> *Samas [Shammash] is before me.*
> *Nanna [Sin] is behind me.*
> *Nergal is at my right hand.*
> *Ninurta is at my left hand.*

Adding to this, the modern *Mardukite* version appends—

Anu, above me, King of Heaven.
Enki, below me, King of the Deep.
The power [blood] of Marduk is within me.
It is not I, but Marduk, who performs the incantation.

The priest mystically sheds singular awareness of his "mortal spark," even if only for a moment—to experience "*transcendental magic*" clad in *godhood*. Direct parallels may be drawn from this rite to others found in "Hermetic" magic and the "Kabbalah." Rising on the planes of perception, awareness and knowing—as a *god*, speaking on behalf of the *Chief* of the pantheon—the magician-priest is now able to influence worldly affairs in the *original* and most powerfully direct "magical" means known—a direct interface with the *gods* as one of their own.

— 14 —
: "ON EARTH, LIFE" :
AKITU—THE BABYLONIAN NEW YEAR

> *"The Babylonian observation of the annual (solar) year starts with the 'Mardukite' observation of Zagmuk—meaning 'the beginning of the year' or 'new year'. This 12-day festival is fixed to arrange its height at the beginning of the month of Nissanu, the 'Spring Equinox' or March 21st, also coinciding with the beginning of the astrological wheel, when the sun enters Aries."*
> ~ Joshua Free
> *The Book of Zagmuk by Nabu*

In ancient *Babylon*, the New Year Festival was the central most religio-political "Mardukite" event marking the beginning of the annual cycle. At that time in "celestial history," the spring equinox observation of *Akitu* (or *Akiti*) coincided with the sun entering the *"Aries"* zone, the zodiacal sign of MARDUK. This spring festival symbolized not only agricultural fertility and renewal of the land on earth, but also a restatement or reinforcement of the national position of MARDUK and his role in the universe.

The Akkadian name for the final day of the festival—*Akiti* or *Akitu*—translates roughly to *"On Earth, Life."* Most scholars usually only recognize the "agricultural" significance and not necessarily the "political" and "mystical" functions of the observation. True, the *Akitu* festival took place twelve days before the annual crops were planted—but, this large public national "celebration" also reconfirmed supremacy of MARDUK and the *Babylonian* Pantheon, making it the single most important ancient "holiday" for the Mardukite tradition. After a time of gods had come and gone, the priests and kings continued to observe these ceremonial customs using representative "images" or statuary to symbolized the "divine presence" of MARDUK and NABU as they made a procession each year through the streets of *Babylon*. [The applicable parallels to "Easter" (*&tc.*) are innumerable as we progress our understanding of the ritual text.]

Each of the twelve festival days begins at dawn. The *High Priest* of the *"Temple of Marduk"*—the E.SAG-ILA or *"House of Marduk"*—goes and prepares the temple and other ceremonial areas before dawn, then makes a "general invocation" to MARDUK, before the "image" (statue) of the *god* in his shrine.

On the first day of the festival, *after* the priests carried out morning services, the King accompanies a procession around the city of *Babylon*, showing the people that he carried the official "royal" regalia of his position—the "*Crown of Anu*," the *Scepter of Dragonblood*, &tc. This is to secure the symbolism of "worldly material reign" firmly in the consciousness of the population. Transfer of this power to the king by the gods demonstrates his "*Divine Right to Rule*." Then, portions of the "*Enuma Elis*" are read to prove that Marduk is authorized to dispense this "divine right."

During the second day, the *High Priest* is charged to ritually cleanse the temple with consecrated waters from both rivers of *Babylon*—the *Tigris* and the *Euphrates*. Sweet *f*ragrances of juniper and cypress fill the air. The official image (statue) of NABU is carried from the nearby city of *Borsippa* and left just outside of *Babylon* at the *Uras Gate*.

The sacred symbols of "worldly material reign" are removed from the King by the *High Priest* and taken by procession to the *Temple of Marduk*, where the symbols are placed before the (statue) feet of the *god*. These "sacred objects" are only "returned" to MARDUK briefly, so that the *Anunnaki King* may dispense them "officially" back to the *Earthly King* who rules the Babylonian nation in the name of MARDUK. This also demonstrates to all concerned that these symbols of reign are only "borrowed" by kings, who are really "stewards" for MARDUK on Earth. The statue of MARDUK is brought outside the *Esagila* and the King makes his appeal to rule before it. Then, the items of power are returned to the King by the *High Priest*, and a procession ensues back to the palace, showing the people that the King has been granted the "Divine Right" by MARDUK.

Day three involves a reenactment of the "*Enuma Elis,*" followed by a procession of the image/statue of NABU on a pathway of reeds. NABU is brought before the Sumerian "*Temple of Ninurta*" (sometimes called the "*Temple of Fifty*") where he is to "defeat" two enemies ("*evil gods*") in the name of MARDUK. A dramatization is performed—two statues are destroyed before his image. NABU is then left at the "*Temple of Ninurta*" until the sixth day of the festival.

On the fourth day, both statues are ritually "cleansed" by the *High Priest*. The image of MARDUK is returned to the *Esagila*, where MARDUK is symbolically "imprisoned within the mountain" (or "pyramid")—which had happened during the fall of the first "Tower of Babel" in prehistory. In one account, he is trapped is by "two evil gods," presumably the same ones that NABU defeats.

A more accurate explanation according to tradition is that his imprisonment was a political punishment for the death of *Dumuzi* (or *Tammuz*)—consort of INANNA-ISHTAR. MARDUK remains "buried alive"—*dead but dreaming*—for three days. During this, on the fifth day, the epic cycle of INANNA-ISHTAR—known as the *"Descent to the Underworld"*—is recited (or dramatized) and NABU finally enters the city again on the sixth day.

Ceremonial applications of the seventh day are derived from a wisdom series, given as the *Book of Nabu-Tutu Tablet-T* series in *"Necronomicon: The Anunnaki Bible."* Here, the young prophet-son deity—NABU—approaches the *voice* of the *"unseen god,"* MARDUK as *Amon-Ra* entrapped in the "pyramid." During the festival, NABU—the statue/image of NABU—is brought before the image of the imprisoned "MARDUK" statue to receive the mysteries from the "unseen god."

A great victory procession of MARDUK and NABU commences on the ninth day. Their statues and those of their consorts—SARPANIT and TESHMET—are cleaned on the tenth day before they are receive a final grand celebratory procession on the eleventh day. Then after the priests conduct closing "consecration" rites at dawn on the twelfth day, the images/statues are retired to their appropriate places and Babylonian work-a-day life returns to normal.

— EPILOGUE —
: A BRAVE NEW BABYLON RISING :
by "Sortiléges" David Zibert

Conflict. . . Unrest. . .

On earth as it is in heaven. . .

At the precipice of a planetary evolution, the *world* ends.

It always does.

Global tensions rise to unprecedented heights with the passing of each day. The *bright future* once wrought for mankind grows dark for the race as a whole. To it: arcane philosophy failed; ageless religion failed; humanistic ideals failed; and every magic spell and scientific formulae furthers sealing mortal man in his own self-made systematic prison, driving the coffin nail home—a single-track to travel upon furthering our journey into the *downward spiral* sending a world into inevitability. . .

. . .*apocalypse.*

And this is my hope for the world, shared from the depth of my soul and joined in the voices of many self-honest truth seekers who have seen for themselves. . . renewal!

The mystics know; the children know; even the *birds* know – the world is *ending*. Of course, this does not imply the blatant physical, material and totalitarian destruction of humans (so let us not employ the same scare tactics of every evangelizing preacher under the sun), it is instead the ending of *a human world*.

Recorded legends on ancient tablets point toward an era of *renewal* that will give way to the fabled *Golden Age*, a *Brave New World*—a true *new age*. But this is no *new* idea at all, rather it is something predicted by the main tenets of every true spiritual path throughout history, differentiated solely by semantics and appearing as varied as opinions from the *Second Coming of Christ* to the the cosmic collapse of the material universe by some rift in space-time or even *dark matter* and *black holes*.

You can label and interpret, even sugarcoat, what is happening any way you like—the simple fact remains: There is an undeniable feeling shared throughout the collective human consciousness that *something* is about to happen—that something *is* happening—and yet it all seems to endlessly cycle back and forth in some determined fragile balance. So *what* are we to do?

While the bungled confusion of the world plagues the mind with anxiety demons and victimization tendencies, the answer couldn't be simpler: *we must provoke the end of the world*, in this case, through a *massive paradigm shift*, meaning the necessary return of the *true spirituality*. By this, I mean the original *stuff*; untainted; undefiled through time by the analytical minds and personal truths of men corrupted into *systems*—fragmented from the whole; never the tween shall meet; *thank you, call back later*. It may seem like nothing new; but *no*, this time *it is different*.

In the wake of this self-honest planetary need for a *Great Awakening*, and on the cusp of a true *new age*, many "cults" have risen in recent past, loosely termed "pagan." Yet, in all of their once revolutionary efforts marked upon human consciousness, what they have to offer is often really only a "turn of the wheel," simply providing a different container for the *same content*, proving to us once again that humanity has not evolved much since the days of antiquity.

Understand we are not here to tell you what to think, raising our "*Mardukite literature*" to some new authoritarian heights, but we are offering critical information and data correction for your noggin so that you might *self-honestly* think for *yourself*. The emphasis here on *self* is not merely some glorification of individualism or newfangled ego-worship, but an affirmation that if we really want to change the *world*, we had better clean up and change our *self* first. When each human being takes the responsibility to grasp the *self-honest* realizations of who they are and where they come from, what the world is and how it was made, of the stuff dreams and stars are made of, the *universe* and *everything*—when the experience of all these things can be done *honestly* from *self,* then the race will see an end to the current melancholy, heinous nonsense that is happening and has been happening for quite some time—a condition that is actually *anathema* to the survival of the very creatures that keep these things the way they are!

The premises we use to chart a *new world* are simple enough:

- *Every* human being has the potential and responsibility to experience life in *self-honesty*.

- *Every* human being has the right and freedom to demand this of their existence.

- *Every* human being has to embrace *some universal oneness* in order to live in harmony with itself as a race of brethren; with the Earth as a base of homestead; and with the universe as a matrix of existence. Only then can humans experience true *unity with all life, the universe and everything!*

This is our *true* and *destined* existence.

But what has kept man from achieving these ends? Why is it that the shortcomings of humanity throughout history seem to keep repeating recursively? Why has *everything* failed? As with all else, we find that the answer is again quite simple: *because humans are forgetful*.

We forget easily; we are often sad; we suffer; we lose sight. To regain anything meaningful for the present and any hope for the future, we must remember what once was, and fortunately for us, an order of some of the earliest mystics thought of just that—so they created *cuneiform-writing*.

This book, as with the remaining "cycle" of literature produced by the "*Mardukites*," is sure to present to you ideas of "history" and "magic" in ways you have never seen, or maybe even imagined before. The tradition that it represents does not deal in rudimentary hierarchical *grimoires* or the application of general hermetic principles upon some historical ethnocentric tradition. The "Mardukite" work runs much deeper than even this. It presents *The System*—the *archetypal* system—that has formed the basis for every mystery tradition to later emerge.

In other words: if you can correctly understand the means and motives of the mysteries and religion of Babylon and Sumer, you will correctly be able to interpret "history" and "magic" as a whole—whatever these words may mean to you. You will become privy to the beauty of the original efforts that have mostly deteriorated with time, probably attaining its lowest evolutionary depths in Christian-controlled medieval Europe – or even in the practices of modern day Jews and Muslims who use religion to shroud political reasons for killing one another. Even more important perhaps, you will become aware of what *really* happened in ancient Babylon, and understand whether or not it really was the *right* way to execute *Divine Order*, and why.

Indeed—the focal point of the modern *Mardukite* movement has never been about bringing back the *verbatim* "Babylonian paradigm" one-to-one, because this would only be the "turn of the wheel" again, and we've already grown dizzy and tired by such ventures. *This time*, it's all about fixing what went wrong, actually fixing the problem of *systems*, the root of all problems really, at the core. When every individual takes up the *Sword of Truth* against the world, executing the *acid test* of *self-honesty* on reality, then no doubt a *new*, better, *upgraded* aeon will really begin for mankind. This, we call: *New Babylon!*

To those who *also* feel called to pursue this with us, we say:

WELCOME HOME!

—PART TWO—
THE SUMERIAN ANUNNAKI

— 00 —
: ABZU :
THE PRIMORDIAL ABYSS

For some, it is far too esoteric to say—the true and actual nature of all existence is an "Infinity of Nothingness." Yet, the most ancient spiritual texts suggest this is so. One may even believe they understand the meaning of the very words *"infinity"* and *"nothingness"*—but there is no guarantee this has been properly relayed in the past. Mysterious lore of the *Abyss* is reflected in mystical accounts from around the globe, spanning the entire evolution of human civilization.

A true understanding of this critical state is paramount to real "mystical" work—what is hidden at the heart of most ancient esoteric spirituality. Secrets of the *Ancient Mystery School* affected all systematized living, including the Sumerians. These "secrets" evolved, giving way to later Chaldeo-Babylonian "systems"—forms of "mysticism" and, dare we call it, "magic." Today, we see renewed interest in these matters among both academic scholars and those in the contemporary New Age. But, since the philosophies of the "Classical" era, shamanic cultures of Europe, or even the Egyptians all seem more "accessible" to the modern *"seeker,"* the deeper and more ancient mysteries of Mesopotamia seem to often fade into shadows. Outside of the original esoteric sects, imaginations of the uninitiated surged passed their historical understanding, and a plethora of traditions and systems diverted from the main well-springs, continuing to deflect consciousness further from truly understanding primordial origins.

On the "Arcane Tablets," the *Primordial Abyss* was originally nameless—an "Infinity of Nothingness." As the latent, unmanifest, potentiality of *"Everythingness,"* the *Abyss* is the "All-Source" for any manifestation of *things* in material existence. This concept was not only abstract to the ancients, it remains in the realm of *esoterica* today. To compensate, "pantheist" philosophers arose to equate universal forces with more tangible concepts—physical places names for beings or "creatures." Originally used to philosophically illustrate examples, such beings and places were *so closely* identified with otherwise esoteric concepts in the minds of the general population, that they were blatantly assimilated in consciousness as direct embodiments of these cosmic forces or principles.

Cuneiform tablets from the priest-scribes of NABU also provide evidence for an ancient belief in an "All-Encompassing Being" *begotten* of "the Abyss and the Primordial Sea." This means the *true infinity* of "nothingness" or what we might call "zero" is actually an *a priori* unity of "infinite aspects of itself" as all possible aetheric space—the "nothingness" and the "spaces between" as "One," "All," or rather, "None." This "formula" is generally represented as *"zero times zero"* or "OO"—the *sign of Infinity*. To quote the English philosopher, George Henry Lewes—If zero "0" is the sign of vanished quantity, then the Infinite "00" is the sign of continuity.

Fundamentally, the beauty and simplicity of the infinite of space and pure potentiality of existence is enough for an "All-Encompassing Being," but this is an almost "static" existence with no forces in movement—quite simply All-is-One (*or none!*) in the universe. This background non-existence is not animated—not manifest—and so requires "motion" for any existence. This was born of duality, but of the highest spiritual intent and not to be confused with some mundane spiritual morality. For it was only by the opposition of the primordial currents of "chaos" and "order"—"No-Thing" and "All-Things"—that the cosmos were causally set in motion with a pendulum-like drive toward constant activity, progression and "unfoldment" that we call "existence." The "unrest" of forces is a necessary condition for "Cosmic Law," "The All" or "One" to exist; fragmented by its very first division—that of "existence" and "naught"—the *first dichotomy.*

The *pure potentiality* of "infinite shape, form and variety, in all time, space and quantity" was difficult to relay in primitive language. However, esoteric interpretation of the most ancient Sumerian semantics of an "All-Being" is best reflected by the original meaning of the word "ILU" in Chaldeo-Babylonian literature. The original concept appeared in Sumerian language as "DIN.GIR," meaning "All-God," but later cultural pantheistic interpretations applied this term to individual personified "gods." The "Babylon" city, nation and culture was actually named in honor of their own spiritual quest—a "re-connection" with this "*Source*" by "ascending" the "Ladder of Lights" or "BAB.ILU"—The Gateway to God, or original "Tower of Babel."

True esoteric meaning was lost in time as the word was equated with "gods." An evolving Mesopotamian language system also associated it to "stars," almost changing the function of *Babylon* in consciousness as the "Doorway to the Stars," or as fictional character Daniel Jackson would prefer, a "Star-Gate." Original symbolism and simplicity of the truth is immediately shattered when enters philosophers, scholars and religious scientists—for we have all-too-easily overlooked a stumbling block when interpreting the most ancient tablets concerning divinity.

As Lenormant explains in *Chaldean Magic & Sorcery*—

> "[For] the idea of ILU was too comprehensive and too vast to receive a very definite exterior form, and consequently [too obscure for] the adoration of the people. The personality of ILU was not clearly defined for a long time; his office and title as "God One" were at first given to ANU, "the ancient god," and the first person of the supreme trinity, which was afterward held to emanate from ILU; the priests did not distinguish the primordial principle from the chief of this trinity."

It is here, from the start of our discourse of the "*Sumerian Anunnaki,*" that a *seeker* must first learn to differentiate the "pantheistic personalities" of cultural mythology from the raw esoteric representations. When we exclusively focus on outward expressions of relative stories and histories, any deeper esoteric truths are shroud in mystery and lost to interpretation. If we were to base our cosmogony on purely Chaldeo-Babylonian accounts, one might be led to assume that ANU is born from ILU directly, and then in many regards becomes one and the same as ILU. Mythological "Order" of the *cosmos* is entrusted to the Sumerian "All-Father" of the *Anunnaki gods* as an embodiment of the same. But, physically and literally, Sumerian tablets do not actually ascribe ANU the position of *a priori* "First Being."

Sumerian mythology is troublesome when concerning names, since many titles can be shared by a single being, and what's worse, these titles often get exchanged between various beings at different times and by different tablet authors. At least three sets of "Divine Union" are found to precede the existence of ANU on many of the Sumerian tablets. These names are transliterated by early Sumeriologists as: ABZU and TIAMAT; MUMMU and LAKMU (or LAHMU and LAHAMU); and, ANSAR and KISAR.

The first pair of names are the most applicable to our current chapter—titles with attributes traditionally associated with the "*Abyss*" (ABZU) and the "*Primordial Sea*" (TIAMAT), which as One, compose "nothingness" and "everythingness." Some interpretations confuse these two principles as the same, but they are not. Where the *Abyss* is an infinity of unmanifest potential, the *primordial sea* is an infinity or recursive continuum of form—the *First Cause*—or the "Law" put in motion as infinite manifestation. [The later "Divine Couples" are intended to represent this "2=0" creative principle of "Order" in the *cosmos*.]

Biblical scholars now have conceded to the idea that the Semitic books, like *Genesis*, are indeed the product of a far more ancient Mesopotamian literary influence. "God," the creator of existence, is found alone and everywhere at once, a *"primordial sea"* washing through an *"infinite abyss."* Samuel Kramer summarizes in his *Sumerian Mythology*—

> *"First was the primeval sea.* Nothing concerning the origin or creation of the primeval sea has as yet been discovered in the available Sumerian texts, and the indications are that the Sumerian sages looked upon the primeval sea as a kind of first cause and prime mover."

In the Babylonian *Enuma Elis* "Epic of Creation," ABZU (or APSU) is the first name given, and to it the trait of "primeval," or else the "one who was from the beginning." This persona is later passed on to the local sun by later philosophers and mythographers. In the rendering from our companion title, *"Necronomicon: The Anunnaki Bible,"* we read—

> *And the primeval APSU, who birthed them,*
> *And CHAOS—TIAMAT, the Ancient One,*
> *Mother to them all.*

And from the bastardized version from the Simon *"Necronomicon"*—

> *And naught existed but the Seas of ABSU,*
> *the Ancient One,*
> *And MUMMU TIAMAT,*
> *the Ancient One, who bore them all.*

Where TIAMAT is listed with ABZU (*"and their waters were as one"*), MUMMU is introduced to us in some versions as a "counselor" or "vizier"—a messenger for the pair. The "Epic" continues, informing us that that the other "Divine Couples" were called into being and/or created. Yet, on some other tablets, the word MUMMU or NAMMU is attributed to an *Anunnaki goddess*, a "pantheistic personification" of a humanoid deity synonymous with abstract cosmic role of TIAMAT. Kramer goes on to illustrate this—

> "The goddess Nammu, written with the ideogram for 'sea' is described as 'the life-mother, who gave birth to heaven and earth' [*ti-ama-tu-an-ki*] (or *ama-palil-u-tu-dingir-sar-sar-ra-ke-ne*, 'the mother, the ancestress who have birth to all the gods'). Heaven and Earth were therefore conceived by the Sumerians as the created products of the primeval sea."

Opening lines of the *"Epic of Creation"* confirm these beings existed *"before the heavens and earth were named,"* meaning before material existence were divided into an ordered existence—for in the beginning was All-as-One, and even in the first creative expression, *"their waters were as one."* The first progression or motion of the creative force was to manifest its "every-thing-ness" and "no-thing-ness"—the all-encompassing universe—distinguished on cuneiform tablets by uniting the most basic Sumerian words for "heaven" and "earth," or else, AN and KI. Literally: "heaven-earth," the Sumerians understood AN-KI to mean "universe"—the entirety of the *cosmos,* both "seen" and "unseen."

These powers are called forth to bare witness and offer aid to every charm and prayer of Mesopotamian magic and religion—

Spirit of the Heavens, Remember!
Spirit of the Earth, Remember!

— 0 —
: TIAMAT :
THE PRIMEVAL DRAGON

The first creature spawned from out of the abyss—the *Cosmic Dragon*—to whom the Sumerians would give no less a title than: "Mother of All Creation." In Hebrew, the word is *"tehom,"* meaning "the deep" or "primordial sea," by which this force receives recognition in the Semitic *Genesis*. In an infinite universe not yet manifest, the *"primeval dragon"*—TIAMAT—is the *"first cause"* made by the Absolute, the first fragmentation from wholeness and oneness into existence—the "Law of ALL" put in motion.

In most ancient mythology, the *primeval dragon* is personified as the "Mother of All Creation." This force, identifiably female, is credited with creation of the other *"gods,"* including all corporeal spirits visible on earth in ancient times as the *"Anunnaki."* This belief found its way into modern "New Age" theories explaining physical aspects of the *gods* as "reptilian" in nature, descended from a "Great Cosmic Dragon." By definition, all existences fall under this *"Cosmic Law"*—all existences are extensions of the same *"Universal Agent."*

The essence of wholeness (or duality in wholeness) is represented in the Mesopotamian pantheon as "divine unions" or couples. Both the male and female aspects are seen as reflections of as one—though like the physical sexes manifest of man, they are divided for our interpretation as being "god" and "goddess." Depending on the tablet sources, the deeds and attributes of one are often placed on the other, demonstrating that the full qualities are complete only when paired. For this reason, early scholars examining the Creation tablets mistook ABZU (*the Abyss*) as literal "consort" of TIAMAT. But after *his* "death," in the Babylonian account, her husband-partner is listed as KINGU.

Let us be clear, however, that more than ABZU, KINGU or any other primordial name listed on pre-Anunnaki lists of "rulership" in heaven, it is the *primeval dragon*—called "TIAMAT"—that is attributed all active ability of creation in the Universe. As the primal force or "prime mover" of a physical existence that came out of the *Abyss*, our first "deity" (if we are to call it such) is not only a dragon, but female, and her consort is given the more passive role for the act of creation.

Under the epitaph of *"Nammu," "Mammu," "Mummu," "Mammi"* or *"Mami"* (of which was later assimilated into the Babylonian goddess ARURU, among others), TIAMAT is the "Creator Goddess" and "Mother of All Mortal Life," offering up her blood (or "sand from her beaches") to be mixed with the "Breath of ENLIL" and "Waters of ENKI" for the creation of human life on earth. The "name" of MUMMU is actually evoked in Babylonian magic—the "Grimoire of Marduk" or "Book of Fifty Names"—derived from the seventh tablet of the *Enuma Elis*. The thirty-fourth name listed is "MUMMU," who as we have said, is sometimes confused with TIAMAT, but is instead her "vizier" or "chief-minister"—the "active messenger principle." From the "Mardukite" perspective, all aspects of the Fifty Names are attributed to the power of MARDUK in *Babylon*—

> "...the power given to Marduk to fashion the universe from the flesh of TIAMAT offers wisdom concerning the condition of life before the creation, and the nature of the structures of the Four Pillars whereupon the Heavens rest."

This active principle—MUMMU—is described both as the "Creator of the Universe" and also the "Guardian to the Gate to the Outside," but is not originally a "power" of MARDUK, by Sumerian standards. Based on what we know concerning Babylonian adaptations of earlier Sumerian literature, the "Fifty Names" adopted by Marduk in their tradition were really names of the fifty preexisting *"Anunnaki gods,"* some of which are actually mentioned in the *Enuma Elis*, playing active roles during the infamous "war in heaven." It is equally possible, on a cosmological level, that these names reflect some fifty "primary elements" composing the *cosmos* at its material inception. The Babylonian *"Epic"* describes the turbulent formation of earth and humans from "star-stuff" using symbolism of a violent battle between MARDUK and TIAMAT. Michanowsky queries in *"Once and Future Star"*—

> "The great riddle is why the primordial sea, which according to Sumerian belief, brought forth the world around us without conflict or confrontation, had suddenly been recast [in Chaldeo-Babylonian literature] in the image of a vicious demon mother who had to be denounced as a menace to law and order and then cruelly destroyed."

With the rise of later generations of gods, a theme of unseating or dethroning the positions of the original and most ancient pantheon took hold. This dualistic viewpoint is most obvious during the Babylonian era, including later Assyrian offshoots.

We see the first militant acknowledgment of a generational gap between the "younger" and "elder" pantheons in the *"Enuma Elis,"* where the "elders" are either demonized as "evil," removed from the system entirely, or given only passing mention. Compared to earlier Sumerian beliefs, this dualism would seem artificial, created for the sole purpose of elevating the position of the younger pantheon, observed in Babylon, as the supreme forces in the local universe and thereby usurping their ancestors. What could not be done physically was accomplished in a manner that ruling classes have used since the dawn of history: the very alteration of said *history*.

Lore of this rebellion is found in post-Sumerian religious and mystical doctrines that identify with a "good versus evil" motif. We see it in the foundations of nearly all later traditions. From Babylon it spread east to Persia and west to Egypt, where its oldest forms are drawn as antagonistic moral dogmas held by Chaldeo-Babylonians, Egyptians and Zoroastrians. The Semitic traditions also inherited this "dualism," as reflected today in contemporary forms of Islam, Judaism and Christianity—all of which are strongly rooted in opposition and polar worldviews. This is found nowhere in ancient Sumer and seems to attach itself later on to the *Primeval Dragon* icon. It is, perhaps, only loosely based on the "Destruction of KUR," understood by modern Sumeriologists only in relation to other known pantheons, as Kramer does—

> "...the monstrous creature which at least in a certain sense corresponds to the Babylonian goddess Tiamat, the Hebrew Leviathan and perhaps the Greek Typhon."

In the more widely known version of the Mesopotamian "Epic of Creation" [translated fully in *"Necronomicon: The Anunnaki Bible"*] we are given an amazing account of how the patron of Babylon—MARDUK—fights and destroys an "evil dragon," TIAMAT. We are spared no gruesome details of the bloody massacre awaiting her, finalized by an execution-styled beheading. We can see parallels of *"god-kings"* rivaling Chaos-Dragons in many later mythologies. However, on the most ancient tablets of Mesopotamia, this is a dramatic "cosmological" event.

After TIAMAT is slain, half of her ("the head") is used to create the *"heavens"* ("AN") and the other half ("the body") is used to create the *"earth"* ("KI")—or, "AN-KI," the manifested universe. Some "astrophysical" interpretations of these tablets inspire belief that the epic describes a "collision theory" for the local solar system, particularly concerning formation of earth and moon.

We must assume that the philosophical minds that so carefully devised the Chaldeo-Babylonian system (which became so important for the Egyptians and other mystical and Semitic cultures) never fathomed that the tablets of their Sumerian ancestors, sometimes predating them by thousands of years, would ever be recovered. It seemed that for a time, evidence for Sumerian civilization did disappear from human consciousness, replaced instead by the *Genesis* offered by Babylonians and later derived Semitic lore. In fact, they were using the same written writing system, the same pantheon, and many of the same cosmological concepts under varying guises. "Superimposition" at a literary level appeared seamless.

It was not until the late 1800's that "Assyriologists" realized that some of the tablets and artifacts excavated from the Middle East were pre-Semitic—from before the *Akkadians*. It is now clear that "proper" formation and order of the primordial universe was adjusted to meet political and spiritual needs of a tribal people rapidly turned metropolitan, raising the position of their local deity to support the famous and widespread influence of *Babylon*. In this case, the "elder gods" or "ancient ones" are overridden by the "younger gods"—those most most accessible in all global mythologies, usually representing planets of the local solar system in every instance.

Putting the physical cosmology of ABZU and TIAMAT aside—as the *Infinity of Nothing* and the *Prime Cause*—the emphasis of the current discourse is primarily on the pantheistic applications to Sumerian *Anunnaki* lore. It is difficult to determine if this "War in Heaven" among sentient "*gods*" did actually take place or if it was only written about later as propaganda to blot out the significance and contribution of their ancestors. Although not necessarily a moral facet, TIAMAT directly represents the *first existence*—the first separation of wholeness from the All-Source. This, in itself, generates a belief for many, in a "fall from grace" or "removal from the Source"—what is really at the heart of all dualism in global religions. This is most obvious in Gnostic lore—which views all physical existence as "evil," contrast to purely non-material "Godly" or spiritual existence.

If realizing that we occupy physical bodies in separation, removed from "God" directly, we can understand how the human psyche might demonize the form "first removed" as the cause of our own fragmentation. Our ability in explaining this awareness on various "levels" in no way condones behaviors of the younger generation of *gods*. But they too, must have experienced the same philosophic and spiritual devastation of this realization —and at an understandably higher degree of comprehension.

Dualistic conflict of "forces" in the universe are a necessary property of its existence in movement, but it is not necessarily subject to the "moral dualism" that humans identify with. Forces are constantly working with and against once another to keep "the organized universe" the way it is—and continually moving to the way it will be. Without this, there is only the static and "Infinite Nothing" existence of the original state of ALL, which we cannot even inhabit and still be separated as a being of *Self*. Thus, the real "division" is essentially what is visible and what is not visible (from "human" perspective)—for the infinitude we inhabit contains everything and nothing can not exist. In Sumerian mythology, this is observed in the union or bond of "heaven-earth" (AN-KI) as a singular aspect; as a dual aspect, the seen and unseen aspects of reality; and as a zero aspect, still encompassed in and of the abyssal nothingness. Sumerians depicted this abstract form as a *"mountain,"* the physical "bond" between "heaven" and "earth." *Ziggurats* were built as a reflection of the same.

We have previously mentioned the "Destruction of KUR" in passing. Not only does the word KUR mean "mountain," but it appears in the only significant "dragon-slaying" example from pre-Mardukite Sumerian literature. This time, however, KUR is not a cthonic abyssal water-based dragon, but is instead deep in the earth, in the mountain—or in a very literal sense, the mountain (earth) itself. There are three available Sumerian versions of this tablet cycle, each successively more recent in its origination, as the characters change.

Kramer conveniently paraphrases the three versions—

> "The first involves the water-god Enki, whose closest parallel among the Greeks is Poseidon. The hero of the second is Ninurta, the prototype for the Babylon god Marduk when playing the role of 'hero of the gods' in the Babylonian Epic of Creation. In the third, Inanna, counterpart of the Semitic Ishtar, plays the leading role. In all three versions, however, the monster being destroyed is termed KUR."

KUR is an obscure enigma for the prehistoric Sumerian pantheistic worldview, which is otherwise orderly and peaceful. Only later with increased human population did disharmony arise, wrought by new traditions of "evil sorcerers" commanding chaotic "demons" of plague and pestilence. But these expressions are merely accelerated entropy in motion—the opposite of growth and nurture. They do not seem to correlate with a dualistic nature of "good versus evil" applied to our lore of the archetypal primeval dragon.

This force only appears chaotic due to its infinite expressions of "change" and "birth"—like the amoral explosive emission of life from seed or egg. Some esoteric texts render TIAMAT as the "Ancient of Days." In the Chaldeo-Babylonian kabbalistic system—also called the *Ladder of Lights*—a mystic confronts TIAMAT ladder as the "Dweller on the Threshold" or "Guardian of the Gate to the Outside"—as a representation of the "Fear of the Unknown" that blocks progress. In other traditions of magic, it is KHORONZON, the "Dragon of Chaos" encountered in the dimensional ascent of astral pathwork.

Modern mystical encounters with this energy may prove challenging for some who hold onto the more animated depictions of a primeval "Dragon of Chaos." This current of power is rather subtle (or gentle) like the waves of the sea, but they can just as easily turn turbulent when perturbed. Anthropomorphic manifestations and astral encounters with a personification of TIAMAT generally reflect her "reptilian" form as a sleek black dragon. Rarely she may assume a more human form, almost resembling Semitic lore of "*Lilith*," but always female, and usually with black hair. In *Babylon*, The Tiamat Gate is essentially the "*Gate to the Outside*," which is to say in more esoterically acceptable terms, the "*Gate to the Abyss*."

— I —
: ANU :
KINGSHIP IN HEAVEN

Literature from the Sumerian tradition—cuneiform tablets unearthed during the last century—reveals that the Anunnaki system is the original archetypal "Olympian" pantheon of deities copied and pasted onto diverse cultures for thousands of years.

The Anunnaki were originally assigned to twelve positions in the cosmos forming a celestial sphere around the earth (later yielding lore of the "zodiac") and to twelve bodies of our local solar system (ten planets, plus the sun and moon). Prior to the "Ammonite" fascination with the local Sun, best observed among the Egyptians and other solar-cults, it was this collective star-system (or "pantheon") that the ancients deemed the "Rulers of Fate" and "Keepers of the Sacred Cycles on Earth"—the cosmic order of the organized universe.

"Ancient Ones" from Sumerian prehistory—ABZU, TIAMAT, LAHAMU, &tc.—are given brief mention in cuneiform literature, but are viewed as more abstract or metaphysical properties of creation, not accessibly appropriate as traditional deities. We have shown in other chapters how such forces could be seen as the primordial essence of the "All-Source" being first made manifest. But the Sumerians also viewed these active properties as materializing in their own personified "All-Father"—ANU—a figurehead for the hierarchical pantheon. These traits or energetic currents of primordial forces are assimilated by successively "younger gods" as they are elevated to higher roles in the hierarchy.

The genealogy given in the *Enuma Elis* "Epic of Creation" depicts ANSAR (or *Anshar*) and KISAR (*Kishar*) as father and mother of AN ("ANU" in Chaldeo-Babylonian). ANU, in turn, is credited as father of both the I.GI.GI—a legion of "celestial spirits" who "watch" and "see"—and AN.UN.NA.KI (or Anunna-Ki, sometimes spelled "Anunna-Ge" by early Sumeriologists)—a pantheon of "gods" who *"decree the fates of earth."* The names ANSAR and KISAR are most coherently translated as "heaven-zone" and "earth-zone" respectively. "SAR" means "cycle" or "the round of" in *Babylonian* language.

If we adhere to this defined cosmology, their division as separate and then unity as wholeness is the progenitive spark producing an archetypal lineage of distinct and sentient gods born directly from the "omni-dimension," first known to itself only as the Abyss, then separated by the Primordial Waters and then finally condensed and separated as "heaven" and "earth." Some folk have put forth the suggestion that the *Anunnaki* actually entered our earthly "time-space" from another dimension or star-system.

Most cuneiform tablets are written very "matter-of-factly," almost reminiscent of technical writing. Their authors felt no need to "validate" or "prove" the existence of the *Anunnaki* any further—just as we today write our own events and history as "statements" that are fundamentally understood within the context of our culture. Naturally, the oldest surviving Sumerian accounts of the "creation of the universe" are sparse and badly fractured. References to AN ("ANU") specifically, are few in number when compared to his later and more active children. While the actually name and power is frequently called upon, very few tablets are dedicated ANU specifically. Rather than petitions for aid, they are often "hymns" of praise, as reflected in this seven-line cuneiform tablet fragment, translated by L.W. King—

> 1. *siptu bilu sur-bu-[u]...*
>   "Mighty Lord..."
> 2. *ilu-Anim sur-bu-[u]...*
>   "ANU, Might Lord..."
> 3. *ilu sami-i...*
>   "God of the Sky..."
> 4. *ilu-Anim ilu sami-[i]...*
>   "ANU, god of the Sky..."
> 5. *pa-sir u-mi...*
>   "Loosener of the Day..."
> 6. *ilu-Anim pa-[sir u-mi]...*
>   "ANU, Loosener of the Day..."
> 7. *pa-sir sunati...*
>   "Interpreter of Dreams..."

As we see in more popular interpretations from the last century, academic scholars have filled in many cracks of these broken tablets with the lore presented in post-Sumerian periods. The farther away from the original simplicity of the tradition that we get, however, the more strongly the Semitic influences and those of Zoroastrian dualism are incorporated. Again, academician have often employed the reverse engineering method of working backwards from more familiar (and relatively more recent) systems in which to interpret antiquated and more obscure ones.

This is purely fallacious, especially given what we commonly know regarding the degradation of information transmission (communication) over time.

It is sometimes difficult to separate the interpretation of ANU's position without conjuring up lore connected to his offspring. Many tablet authors began their sagas and incantations with some kind of unifying genesis to support why such and such happened or where such a such draws their power from, like the following, translated by Kramer—

> *After heaven had been moved away from the earth,*
> *After earth had been separated from the heavens,*
> *After the name of man had been fixed;*
> *After AN had carried off heaven,*
> *After ENLIL had carried off earth,*
> *After ERESHKIGAL had been carried off into KUR as its prize...*

Following sequential logic of the above passage, unity of creation fractured into dual existence of "heaven" and "earth," which were then separated from one another. In this ancient Sumerian version, AN "carries" off heaven, becoming responsible for the organization and order of heaven, and his son ENLIL is left to oversee work concerning physical existence on Earth. [And in this instance, "KUR" is used synonymously as "*Underworld.*"]

Later Assyrio-Babylonian or "*Mardukite*" versions attribute more of these responsibilities to the lineage of ANU's *other* son, ENKI (or EA) and his son, MARDUK—figures receiving little attention in the purely Sumerian sources, also for political reasons.

The position of ANU in the Sumerian pantheon is as an undisputed "*Father in Heaven,*" who acts as the supreme "progenitor" or "father of the gods" from his place as the "King of the Local Universe." The "*House of Anu*" (the traditional "heaven" or "abode of the gods") is sometimes written as UR.ANU or "*Uranus*" (from the Greek "*Ouranos*"). His most sacred place of "worship" on earth was in the city of Uruk at the temple of E.ANNA—also translated to mean "*House of Anu.*"

The number of his rank is sixty—the number of cosmic perfection, or "whole value," in Mesopotamian mathematics—similar to our "100," but expressed in their entire mathematical system in a manner similar to our own retention of their division of a *whole hour* by *sixty* minutes, not *one-hundred*.

Later Mesopotamian traditions viewed ANU in a similar manner as the abstract Babylonian expression of ILU. He became the "Lofty One" or "Supreme God Most High" in the pantheon, a remote, distant and indiscriminate All-Father much more representative of the "Heavenly Father" that Jesus alluded to in the *New Testament* then that of the *Old Testament* God of the Hebrew. Solidity of his personification becomes increasingly faint in descending traditions, and though within his power, he rarely intervenes or makes an appearance to the "earth" world of gods and men. His main function in the pantheon is as the "Father" of the gods, who are then mainly left to deal with material universe on their own accord.

> When first the gods were [like] men on earth,
> Settling on the bond-heaven-earth,
> ANU decreed the *Anunnaki* would come forth...
> —Tablet A, "Necronomicon: The Anunnaki Bible"

Few incantation tablets (or "prayers") invoke the powers of Anu directly. The heavenly force is perceived as too vast to be channeled directly by successors and to degrade it to anything more accessible would be to compromise the nature of what is represented. In Semitic traditions, the role of Kingship in Heaven is equated to the full extent of power that keeps the universe in motion, contained in an "unspeakable" and "unknowable" name (termed "Tetragrammaton" in modern Hebrew-based mysticism—YHVH). It is more common for the magician, priest or priestess to evoke a subsidiary deity from the "pantheon" ("*divine lineage*") to invoke the names known to them rather than pursue methods of Egypto-Hermetic cryptomancy to divine and compel spirits against their will using "true-names." In the Chaldeo-Babylonian tradition, the names of ENKI and MARDUK are evoked to speak the names —later traditions often used them to replace obscure and "secret" names altogether. As Lenormant explains—

> "True indeed there was a supreme name which possessed the power of commanding the gods and extracting from them a perfect obedience, but that name remained the inviolable secret of *Hea* or EA—ENKI. In exceptionally grave cases the magician besought *Hea*, through the mediator *Silik-mulu-khi*—MARDUK, to pronounce the solemn word in order to re-establish order in the world and restrain [temper] the powers of the abyss. But the enchanter did not know that name, and could not in consequence introduce it into his formulae... he could not obtain or make use of it.

He only requested the god who knew it to employ it, without endeavoring to penetrate the terrible secret himself."

Though appearing infrequently in prayers, one example of a magician's "Grand Invocation" addressing ANU appears as a protective incantation at times and then also a hymn of adoration.

From *Tablet-P* in "*Necronomicon: The Anunnaki Bible*"—

> ANU, King in Heaven, Eternal Prince of the *Anunnaki*,
> Whose words are the rule over the *Assembly of Anunnaki*,
> Lord of the unequaled Horned Crown [*of the Starry Heavens*],
> You who can travel anywhere in the universe on a raging storm;
> You who stands in the royal chamber admired as a king.
> The ears of the IGIGI are directed to hear your pure words,
> The *Assembly of Anunnaki* gather around thee in reverence.
> At your command the *Anunnaki* bow to salute;
> At your command the wind blows
> And food and drink are abundant;
> At your command the angry demons
> Turn back to their habitations.
> May all the gods of Heaven and Earth
> Pray at your *Altar of Offering;*
> And may the kings of dragonblood on Earth
> Give you heavy tribute.
> May men pray to you daily and offer sacrifices and adoration.
> May your heart be at rest and may you ever reign righteously.
> To the city of *n.* show your abundant favor and grace."

The no less significant role of royal "Lady of Heaven" does not appear to be fixed individual. Several female entities are listed at one time or another as consorts of ANU. The title-name ANTU is usually given, and much like the name of her husband, her title is more of a role than a proper name (and carries a numerological designation of 55). The "Queen of the Starry Heavens" traditionally rules the cosmos with her partner, but the exact personality associated often it differs by tradition.

In one interpretation of the Sumerian *Genesis*, the consort of ANU (or AN) is originally listed as KIA (or KI), the "*Spirit of the Earth*" that "ENLIL separated from the heavens." In a rather romantic Babylonian version, ANU bestows the name of I.STAR or *Ishtar* (Sumerian: IN.ANNA)—meaning "beloved of ANU"—onto his grand-daughter, a title-position sharing that of his own consort.

If one were to assume that the ANShAR and KIShAR [parents to AN and KI] represents the pure spirit of *zi-an-na* (spirit of heaven) and *zi-ki-a* (spirit of earth) in the mystical incantations, then we might assume, since not otherwise addressed from the pantheon, that the addendum nearly always added in prayer to the forces (after those just mentioned) are to the manifested "first forms" of both heaven and earth as *zi-dingir-anna* and *zi-dingir-kia*. KANPA is translated from our original "*Mardukite*" cypher manuscript [*Tablet-I* in "*Necronomicon: The Anunnaki Bible*"] as either "mark well," "remember" or "conjure" based on references from the last two centuries of revived tablet literature. DINGIR is given as "first-god" or "mighty spirit power."

> *Zi Anna Kanpa*
> *Zi Kia Kanpa*
> *Zi Dingir Anna Kanpa*
> *Zi Dingir Kia Kanpa*

Mystical experiences by modern Mardukites with ANU directly have been limited. Given the archetypal sage-hermit motif attached to him, it can be difficult for the mind to comprehend the force of his "shade." Though it may be the result of poetic licensing, his image of a "King in Heaven" seated on a throne in the clouds can be traced back even to these first spiritual philosophies. Whether or not this is taken literally by an initiate, the fact remains that according to tradition, ANU leads the original *Anunnaki* pantheon of Sumerian "elder gods" to earth. For meditations and modern ritual, his sign is often traced as a singular ray (or arrow bolt) descending downward.

— II —
: ENLIL :
DEMIURGE OF CREATION

After the realms of "heaven" and "earth" had been clearly defined, the great separation or fracture of reality ensued. In fact, the ancient texts quite literally describe this as the heavens (the eternal all-encompassing space aspect) being "moved away" from earth (the solidified concentrated matter aspect). This is generally followed by a reiteration—ancient tablet writers seemed to enjoy poetic redundancy—of earth being "separated" from heaven, as evident even in the *"Song of the Hoe"*—

> *ENLIL, who will make the human seed of the Land*
>   *come forth from the Earth,*
> *and not only did he hasten to separate heaven from earth,*
> *and hasten to separate earth from heaven...*

It is customary for Sumerian tablet cycles to begin with the formation of creation and the genealogy of their pantheon even if it did little to contribute to the actual context of the saga. It is possible that this literary mechanism added credibility epic characters and places set against the background reality of creation, and of course, the *"gods."* The act may also have been a result of devotion and respect. In parody we might equate this to—*"First the universe was created, then the gods were born and then such and such happened."*

Many of early tablet cycles include introductory lines that reinforce an understanding of Sumerian cosmogony and spirituality. Judging by the frequency of their appearance, there is little doubt concerning the identity of at least two primary gods of the Sumerian tradition, the first of which we have already mentioned—

> *After AN had carried off heaven*
> *After EN.LIL had carried off earth*

EN.LIL—["EN"=*Lord*, "LIL"=*Air, Breath, Lofty*]—was the national god of ancient Sumer, essentially displacing (the more distant and less materially concerned) AN (ANU) as head of the "Elder Gods" on Earth. ENLIL's offspring include the majority of the "younger generation" of *"Enlilite"* gods.

His "patron-city" or "sacred-city" was Nippur [NI.IBRU], named for the geographic center (or "mid-section") of Mesopotamia, where his temple-ziggurat was built—the E.KUR, "House [like a] Mountain"—the four corners of which represented the quarters of the material world. His consort is also ranked high in the pantheon—NIN.LIL (or in the later form as *Belit*)—a title given to SUD. ENLIL's position is designated 50—"Command of Physical Space"—in Mesopotamian numerology, and the correlating rank for NINLIL is 45.

More than simply a "Ruler" of the Organized Universe, ENLIL's position and title displays him as the original representation of the *"demiurge"* of creation—best known as a "Gnostic" concept, borrowed from Greek and Hermetic Schools—meaning the "designer of the material world" (a title also attributed to ENKI as *Ptah*, "the Engineer," in Egypt). But, ENLIL did not personally attend to each and every aspect of this material world. His commanding position enabled him to focus on *management—overseeing* other "spirits," "angels" or Anunnaki that were led down from the "heavens" (or, out of an inter-dimensional existence, *&tc.*) to forge a concrete physical existence on "earth"—like adding paint to a once blank canvas of infinite potentiality. For this, he is the *first* attributed with the power of the number "Fifty," also the number of names (of "angelic" war-generals, bio-engineers, *&tc.*) found on the seventh tablet of the *Enuma Elis*. This is the same "Power of Fifty" attributed as the "names" of MARDUK in *Babylon*, used to elevate him to the position of "Enlil-ship" [*ell-ilu'tu*] or "Kingship" of the material world.

ENLIL's first responsibility in the "new world" was assigning tasks and official designations, some of which seem to have been competed for. Sumerian tablets account for one such instance, introducing us to the forerunners of Cain and Abel, two brothers who rival against one another in an agricultural contest to win the favor of ENLIL and the position of "farmer-god." Given the peaceful "swords to plow-shares" described in literature from ENLIL's *Sumer*, no bloody murder is described at the climax of the story, but instead a simple judgment by "wise father ENLIL," which is mutually agreed upon by the the two brothers (Emesh and Enten) and they toast one another with libations! The translation by Kramer—

> ENLIL answers *Emesh* and *Enten*:
> "The life-producing water of all the lands,
> *Enten* is its 'knower,'
> As farmer of the gods he has produced everything.
> *Emesh*, my son,
> How dost thou compare thyself with *Enten*, thy brother?"

> The exalted word of ENLIL whose meaning is profound,
> The decision taken, is unalterable,
> Who dares transgress it?
> *Emesh* bent the knees before *Enten*,
> Into his house he brought . . . [offerings],
> The wine of the grape and the date.
> *Emesh* presents *Enten* with gold, silver and lapis lazuli.
> In brotherhood and friendship,
> Happily, they pour out libations,
> Together to act wisely and well, they determined.
> In the struggle between *Emesh* and *Enten*,
> *Enten*, the steadfast farmer of the gods,
> Having proved greater than *Emesh* . . .
> . . . O father ENLIL, praise!

Another ancient Sumerian epic—the Creation of the Pickax—describes the agricultural tool ENLIL gave to the "primitive workers" to aid their fieldwork, keep the populations fed, but also to ensure appropriate offerings of sustenance were being brought to the temple-ziggurats. As a deity in the Anunnaki Pantheon, ENLIL's role and identity is best reflected in the purely Sumerian texts. He is transferred to the Babylonians as IL.LIL, to the Assyrians as *Bel* (the original one, anyway) and he even becomes the prototype of the Semitic Yahweh (EL in Hebrew).

None of these later forms actually preserve the definitions of his position among the original Sumerians—"Lord God" of the Judeo-Christian *Old Testament*, as Lenormant confirms—

> "*Hea* [EA–ENKI] passed into the Chaldeo-Babylonian [system] without changing his office, character or name, (but) *mul.ge.lal* [ENLIL], on the contrary, bore no resemblance in the documents of the magical collection to [his former office] *Bel*, demiurge and god of the organized universe, with whom he was afterward assimilated, in order to find him an equivalent in the religion by which he was adopted."

An apparent dualism later emerged in Mesopotamia, not only between lineages of ENLIL and ENKI, but also among political campaigns of the "younger" gods. This "philosophical conflict" is all too easily passed off in people's mind's as "light versus dark" and "good versus evil." But, what we are really given is a "division of reality"—still a singular reality mind you, but divided in consciousness.

The *demiurge* of creation is later viewed as the "separator" of the *physical* from the *spiritual* and thus, by mortal standards, the one responsible for manifesting a world of form that is experienced in pain and suffering. While this is not directly reflected in Sumerian spirituality, the evolution of this esoteric tradition later in Mesopotamia (and elsewhere) accompanied a significant analytical (or critical) thought process with subsequent generations. Each had the opportunity to assimilate and revise the system. Sandra Tabitha Cicero summarizes this development—

> "*Ellil* was a friend to humanity. However, like the Hebrew god *Yahweh*, his anger could be aroused by human wickedness It was *Ellil* who advocated that gods unleash the Great Flood upon humanity in the story of *Atra-Asis*. The unpleasant task of enforcing human calamities decreed by the gods fell upon *Ellil*. Because of this he has usually been accused of being a severe and destructive deity by later scholars. By contrast, Sumerian hymns venerate him as a gracious father figure who protects his people."

Kramer translates an example of such a hymn from the "ENLIL in the E.KUR" tablets—

ENLIL,
Whose command is far reaching;
Whose "word" is lofty and holy;
Whose pronouncement is unchangeable;
Who decrees destinies unto the distant future. . .
The Gods of Earth bow down willingly before him;
The Heavenly gods who are on Earth
Humble themselves before him;
They stand faithfully, according to instructions.
Lord who knows the destiny of The Land,
Trustworthy in his calling;
ENLIL, who knows the destiny of Sumer,
Trustworthy in his calling;
Father ENLIL,
Lord of all the lands;
Father ENLIL,
Lord of the Rightful Command;
Father ENLIL,
Shepherd of the Black-Headed Ones. . .
From the Mountain of Sunrise

> To the Mountain of Sunset,
> There is no other Lord in the land;
> You alone are King.

We see very little of this venerated mention of ENLIL specifically within Mardukite literature of the Chaldeo-Babylonian paradigm. When he is respectfully mentioned, it is usually only in the context of the fundamental "Supernal Trinity" [ANU–ENLIL–ENKI] invoked at the head of some incantations. Most post-Sumerian negative attitudes toward ENLIL centrally focus on his recorded opposition to the creation of humans, and then their preservation during the *Deluge*.

Modern Mardukite experiences with the ENLIL-current are subject to self-honesty. Expectations and culturally based biases held firmly in the psyche will have a hold on any literal interpretations. But this is no less present pertaining to mystical work, which requires the magician maintain an degree of absolute purity and self-honesty if "invoking" this energy. This is the very real "god," depicted in the Judeo-Christian *Old Testament*, and is not trivial being. [In other words: weigh your heart against a feather first!] The mystical symbol most with ENLIL is a downward pointing triangle—a sign of command—possibly a literal representation of energetic flow (downward from above), or else the leadership and power of the Anunnaki "brought down" to Earth.

— III —
: ENKI :
LORD OF THIS WORLD

The spirito-mystical "Supernal Trinity" composing the most ancient pantheon is concluded with ENKI, brother of ENLIL. Anunnaki genealogy records kept by post-Sumerian civilizations emphasize that ENKI and ENLIL are actually half-brothers. Both are divine sons of ANU—the "Sky-Father"—but as royal heir to "Kingship of Heaven," ENLIL is also the son of ANTU—the "official" consort of ANU—while ENKI is born to NAMMU. [Other texts reveal ENLIL as the eldest son of KI and ENKI as the son of ANTU.]

Differing Anunnaki lineages play a more significant role among the "younger pantheon" and later dualistic interpretations, but in the original formation of Sumerian civilization, ENLIL and ENKI are actually perfect compliments to one another in the division of the material world—ENLIL as the ruler of the air and fire aspects, leaving ENKI the domains of *The Deep*: water and earth.

As the original title suggests, "ENKI" means, quite literally, "Lord of the Earth"—["EN"=*Lord*, "KI"=*Earth*]— later known as the Babylo-Akkadian epitaph "EA," likely derived from the Sumerian ideograms for "*house*" [E] and "*water*" [A]. This water alignment is suggested further by names for his temple-ziggurat, built in the southern city of *Eridu* [or *e-ri-dug*—"Home of the Mighty"] known as both E.ENGURRA ("House of Lower Waters") or E.ABZU ("House in the Depths").

Where ENLIL is given a certain authority over the organization of "space" and management of other deities, ENKI is given control over more "worldly matters" on Earth, and carries the designation of 40. [NINKI or DAMKINA, his consort, is 35.] On a cosmological level, ENLIL represents the active spirit manifest in the world as a whole—or the *why*—separated from the "heavens." By comparison, ENKI represents more passive elements, but clearly the more condensed "material" ones solidified on Earth, and also the spirit of *how* things exist—"hidden" internal engineering, program or "natural design."

> "Here in *Eridu* there was a local deity by the name of *Ea*, and the aspiring theologians of that city, eager to make him the supreme deity of the land, pressed forward the claim for lord-

ship over the earth, and in an effort to insure his claim applied to him the epithet *en-ki*, 'Lord of the Earth,' which then became his Sumerian name. But though *Enki*, after some centuries, did succeed in displacing *Ninhursag* [*Belit, &tc.*] and taking third place in the pantheon, he failed to topple *Enlil* from his supremacy and had to settle and had to settle for second best, becoming an *Enlil-banda*, a kind of 'Junior Enlil.' Like other gods he had to travel to *Nippur* to obtain *Enlil*'s blessing after he had built his his temple *E'engurra* in *Eridu*; he had to fill the *Ekur* of *Nippur* with gifts and possessions so that *Enlil* might rejoice with him; though he had charge of the *Me* controlling the cosmos and all civilized life, he had to admit that these were turned over to him by a generous and more powerful *Enlil*."

—S.N. Kramer, *"Sumerian Mythology"*

A Babylonian priest, Berossus, in the 13th Century B.C. wrote an epic dedicated to the figure *"Oannes,"* a later name for ENKI. Here, the author describes ENKI establishing the material infrastructure of human civilization, depicted as the "sublime fish god" [*fish = scales = reptilian*] who rises from his ocean home (or in this case, the Erythian Sea near the Persian Gulf) to teach men the crafts necessary for their developmental arts and sciences to flourish. ENKI is known in *Babylon* as the "Arch-Magus," father of the occult arts and divination, who passed this knowledge to his son, MARDUK. He served as a patron to those who chose spells and esoteric sciences for combat and is sometimes credited with the original knowledge of magical warfare in the local universe. In some Chaldeo-Babylonian mystical texts, ENKI is referred to as "Our Father" in much the same way that the Sumerians referred to ENLIL and, of course, the much later generation of Mardukites (in the neo-Babylonian period) referred to MARDUK.

Similar properties of ENKI described in the *Oannes* saga also appear in another tablet cycle, of Babylonian origin—"The World Order of Enki." [Given on Tablet-K of *"Necronomicon: The Anunnaki Bible."*] Here, the cuneiform author sets out to list the many innovations of ENKI, some of which are originally attributed to ENLIL in earlier Sumerian mythology. Since "Mardukite" Babylonian Tradition recognized MARDUK as ENKI's successor, the finale of the "World Order" tablet concerns the "passing over" of INANNA-ISHTAR for a position among ENKI's roll-call of Babylonian gods. ENKI answers INANNA by documenting implied and bestowed powers she already possesses—but elsewhere from *Babylon*, such as in *Egypt* as ISIS—

What did I keep from you?
What more could we add to you?
You were put in charge of the crook,
The serpent-staff,
The wand of shepherd-ship.
You interpret the oracular omens of battles and combats.
INANNA, you have destroyed what cannot be destroyed;
And you have conceived the inconceivable.

A duality between divine brothers—ENLIL and ENKI—played a significant role in the establishment of not only human civilization in its physical, fundamental and evolutionary aspects, but also the spiritual and religious philosophies that later emerged on the planet. To point out a widely held, but relatively recent conception (adopted by the Roman Catholic Church): "Yahwist Monotheism." This dictates everything in the universe results from a single being alone, the leader of the "*anakim*" or "*malachim*" [*Anunnaki*] appearing in the Judeo-Christian *Old Testament*. The stature of his being is held above all others who are but intermediaries in the stories.

The position in *heaven*, however, seemed too surreal for accessibility by the priests and prayers of early people, so the pantheists and materialists developed patronage toward the "Lord of the Earth"—representing the powers of the *here and now*, and the necessities and comforts of physical existence: fertility, love, wealth... these all became the domain of ENKI, whose "secondary" birthright in heaven seems to have transferred to a "primary" one on Earth.

Trailing in the wake of the gods was their sense of "supremacy"—an embedded pyramid-structure turned innate—first used to govern themselves and then left to chosen figureheads and bloodlines on Earth thereafter. This struggle for world domination and power essentially crippled contemporary humans, who simply do not carry enough awakened genetic and intellectual faculties to properly execute such ventures.

What efforts have been done in the past, both political and physically combative, have been performed by individuals who actually take these matters very seriously. An investigation into the occult beliefs of the Third Reich will reveal that the Nazis actually adopted very similar beliefs concerning the origins of their race and even connected the Germanic interpretation of the Anunnaki pantheon to the Kings of "*Atlantis*"—meaning they believed in higher minds remaining from a prior civilization.

While it does not condone the actions taken, this fueling belief in "god-blood" and "alien-technologies," however trite it might seem to some readers, allowed Nazi Germany to nearly take over the world. We can see some evidence of this "self-righteousness" throughout history. Many folk have felt as if they were direct physical counterparts acting on behalf of their personal god. The very bloodlines of these gods were believed to flow in the veins of certain kings and temple-priests other lineages, thus representing the power attributed to "heaven," but on "earth." Long before World War II, the Christian Crusades of the Middle Ages were fueled by the same belief—that their god had come in human form and bestowed a decree that "on earth as it is in heaven." Suddenly, "Lord of the Earth" became a highly coveted position, for it was now (from an earthly perspective) just as good as that in "heaven" and more immediately accessible to the people. Titles, icons, powers and attributes of the gods, growing more and more distant in memory with the passage of time, were passed on to specific "royal" and "magical" families—the living embodiments of the "old gods" for Earth's future.

As the age of gods passed into a time of men, the harmonic dance of grace and beauty once driving a unified Sumer was gone forever, lost to the variegated mix of analytical minds. "Lordship" passed to the humans—peace and love all but disappeared from the earth. Rivalry for supremacy in a post-Sumerian world of monotheism resulted in many "tribal" wars in the names of their personal deities.

The essence of brotherly love that formed the very systems of physical existence (now being fought over), became separated as "moral dualism"—there was only room for one god now, and the fight for such once political, turned bloody. Of the two brothers, "God" would be associated with all that was orderly, and a "Satan" figure to represent all that was disharmonious. The force of Chaos, first overcome by the Sumerian gods and later tempered to balance creation was now viewed as a source of "evil" and the personification of such was passed onto a "devil," but originally the *brother* of "God."

As Semitic peoples near Mesopotamia developed their own traditions, beneficial properties of the Anunnaki, coupled with the personality of ENLIL, became the figure *Yahweh*. [Yet, the name "EA" clearly has a more similar sound to "*Ia*" or "*Jah*."] The role of *antithesis* was given to ENKI. Although this association of "evil" and "discordance" is hardly justified, the ENKI current energetically assimilated this in consciousness—quite simply, he was now the "rebel" among the "elder" pantheon, and it is not surprising that his most famous offspring—MARDUK—would be a "rebel" son.

As a patron, when all of the other gods have said "no," ENKI is the one that might (almost always) say "yes." This is demonstrated not only in the infamous Flood epic (when he went against the will of the *Anunnaki* to secretly preserve his own bloodline), but in any instance when even the gods are petitioning for favors that the others "won't touch."

For magical purposes, many of ENKI's attributes have since been passed onto the younger generation but in times of extreme need, ENKI seems to be unparalleled in the ability to "get things done – no matter how." He also seems to allot special time and care for INANNA-ISHTAR in several tablet-cycles, including her own infamous epic—"*The Descent.*" But while rebellious, he was no shady rogue: he was a scientist and philosopher above all else, and the greatest of both among the Anunnaki (additionally a child of ANU), his skills and bloodline were prized in the "*fashioning*" of the material world—a title he carried in the Egyptian pantheon as PTAH, the "*designer.*"

The mystical symbol used by modern Mardukites to represent the energetic current of ENKI closely resembles a pyramid or mountain—the KUR. Direction of energy suggested by the symbol is "upward." Movement pools at the surface (or building below the surface of the earth) and is directed towards the sky. It is the exact (polar) opposite to the sign used to represent ENLIL. Both ENKI and MARDUK are, at times, depicted as residing within a chamber, pyramid or inhabiting the "*Deep*" [Abyss], all of which are indicative of an "underverse" operating beneath the surface of consciousness and (visible) material reality.

Modern "Mardukite" encounters with the ENKI-current have been "strong" due to increased modern inclinations of those interested in magic and esoteric sciences. His archetype remains among the most potent alive in systems today. Where the magician is ever seeking the essence of creation or the "words" by which it can be known, in Mardukite tradition, ENKI is considered that very "*word*" of god made manifest and set free to evolve and unfold in the physical world. Fragments of this spiritual understanding are still maintained in the Semitic Kabbalah—lore which is, even in itself, derived from the original Sumerian Anunnaki "*Tree of Life.*"

— 1 —
: NANNA-SIN :
THE MOON – "WHO SHINES FOR"

NANNA is listed on Sumerian tablets as eldest of the "younger pantheon," first-born son of ENLIL and NINLIL. His patron city was Ur, where he maintained primary residence at his temple-ziggurat—E.GISH.NU.GAL or *E.Gishshirgal*—"Home of the Throne Seed." He also made frequent appearances in the northern city of *Harran*, where his *E-Khulkhul* temple stood. NANNA is named for the bright light of the moon gracing the night sky earth, referenced in one epithet as NAM.RA.SIT (*Namrasit*)—"Who Shines Forth." His consort—NINGAL or *Nikkal*—is the "Great Lady of the Moon," goddess of divination and dreams, the most commonly accessible human "thresholds" to interact with the "*Other.*"

NANNA is credited for prosperity of the ancient Sumerian city of Ur. The early metropolis represented the pure idealism of Sumer as brought to high esteem, long before its legendary destruction from the wrath of ANU and ENLIL. Our ancestors preserved details of these events on cuneiform tablet cycles called "lamentations." The famous "Lamentation for the Destruction of Ur" is written from the perspective of the "*Lady of Ur,*" or NINGAL—the consort of NANNA. She relays the sudden sadness that befell the land the day of the "storm" neared. She sheds tears before AN and ENLIL that her city "not be destroyed." But, the assembly of Anunnaki remained *unmoved*—

> *AN never bent toward those words,*
> *And ENLIL never with, 'It is pleasing, so be it!'*
> *[To] soothe my heart.*

ENLIL called down the "storm of heaven" using the "fire-god"—GIBIL—to assist. The gods "left the city ruin and the dead were piled up." In despair, NANNA appeals to his father ENLIL, asking him to lift this heavy curse and restore the city to its former glory. He speaks of the greatness of Sumer and the love for the people toward their gods. But ENLIL is firm, as Thorkild Jacobsen translates—

> *O noble NANNA, be thou (concerned) about yourself,*
> *What truck [sway] have you with tears?*
> *There is no revoking a verdict,*
> *A decree of the assembly,*

> *A command of AN and ENLIL is not known to ever have changed.*
> *Ur was verily granted kingship – an (ever)lasting [eternal] reign,*
> *It was not granted.*
> *You, my NANNA, do not worry. Leave your city!*

This is an abrupt introduction for our character description of NANNA, but it demonstrates the immediate unrest ensuing in Sumer when control is passed to the "younger generation" of *Anunnaki*. The specific reason for the "Destruction of Ur" is conveniently concealed from the tablet saga. Zecharia Sitchin has put forth an interesting theory: Since NANNA is also known as SU.EN (or "SIN" of later Chaldeo-Babylonian literature), it is possible that he either shares an identity with, or lord over, ZU, a "creature" that once stole the "Tablets of Destiny" from ENLIL's possession. That name could self-implicate NANNA as "Lord Zu," or, again, be a reference to control of a serpent-being as EN.ZU—"Lord of the Zu." The name SU.EN might be associated with ZU.EN, or else EN.ZU. The typical persona of NANNA as a "gentle father" doesn't appear to match this allocation. It would, however, provide some explanation for why retributive annihilation came down through the leading pantheon, as city-states started to be governed by the "younger generation."

NANNA is given the number 30, correlating to the lunar month—the word "month" is named for the "moon"—and his consort is 25. As eldest of the "zonei" or "younger pantheon" given control of the local solar-system, NANNA was given the most prominent celestial domain in conjunction with the earth—the Moon. NANNA is actually a shortened version of the more complete designation—Nannar, "Light of the Full Moon." As the form of "SU.EN," he is actually representing the crescent or partial moon, and the Babylonians adopted the name "SIN" from this. The other name "ENZU" is derived from his Akkadian epithet—EN.I.ZUNA—so, the theory mentioned previously is not without some basis.

In Sumerian mythology the moon is held in high regard. Although the primordial chaos cosmologically brings forth the Sun into existence first, as illustrated in nearly all other solar-oriented "Mardukite" systems, the Sumerian Anunnaki chose to represent the Moon with NANNA, a firstborn son of ENLIL and NINLIL, who with his consort NINGAL, give birth to both INANNA-ISHTAR (*Venus*) and SHAMMASH (*the Sun*). It is here, as before concerning cosmology represented by pantheistic beings, that we must keep a distinction between the *Anunnaki* "younger pantheon" and the literal "celestial bodies" they are named for. Ancient tablets are quite obscure in this regard, because cuneiform signs for the planets and deities are identical.

The people, themselves, were not confused by their own tradition, as we might be today when looking back at the tablet records with modern eyes. In one sense, NANNA is described as the "light of the moon." But certainly NANNA, the *Anunnaki King of Ur*, was present in his city while simultaneously the light of the moon bore down on the earth at night. The association is clearly a reference to a more ancient cosmogony reflected in Sumerian beliefs: the day was born from the night, and not that the moon literally gave birth to the sun-star of our local system.

As a mystical "energetic current," the *Moon Gate* is traditionally the first that an individual will encounter when crossing the veils of material existence to the veils of negative existence, or the *Abyss*. Ancient Anunnaki denizens of the universe established "veils of existence" when the "material order" was brought or willed into being. They stationed the "younger pantheon" as *Guardians of the Gates*. The moon, as we might expect, is quite vibrant but gently passive and tranquil. NINGAL—the "Lady of the Moon"—receives many of the lunar attributes in later systems—If not by name, then by gender, as most esoteric revivals that do not truly use the combined-counterpart paradigm of a male-god and female-goddess as one essence, usually reduce celestial divinity to polar dualism: a 'masculine' "solar" god and the 'feminine' "lunar" goddess. But, *Sumer*, unlike *Babylon*, was a primarily *lunar*-oriented tradition with subsequent emphasis on the *Sun* and *Venus*. Ancient astronomical symbols found on the oldest Sumerian art are frequently representations of the *Sun-star, Venus* and, in the case of NANNA-SIN and NINGAL—the *lunar crescent*—which, when depicted above a deity, was often called the "horns."

* * *

Once an "initiate" passes the *"Earth Gate"* in search of cosmic truth on the path of "Ascension" up the *Ladder of Lights*, the lunar current is generally the first one accessed. This is because the "Moon Gate" is most closely aligned to the familiar astral and dreams "level" of enchantment and fantasy that many access—even unknowingly. As an elementary aspect of all mystical work, the "first degree" is where a seeker is able to actually realize in consciousness that they are not only their physical body. Actualization of this basic principle is not taken for granted, since many do not achieve even this "degree" of spiritual evolution (or "unfoldment") during their lifetime. Yet, in contemporary "new age" traditions, many initiates too often simply stop here, even when they believe they have moved on from it, remaining enamored with the infinite potentiality of appearances able to manifest through dissolution of the first veil. Instruction from *"Necronomicon: The Anunnaki Bible"* reiterates—

> "The first 'level' encountered (aside from the extraordinarily subtle or blatantly physical 'Earth Gate') in the system is the Moon Gate, which ironically, is the embodiment of the 'common' astral plane or dreamscape that many have already enjoyed lucid access to without even formal occult education."

The formal "magical path" has a starting point. A magician working through the "veils of existence" connected to and surround us as the systematic design that keeps the material world "flowing." But, be warned: the opiate-like tranquility that the mind can experience at this level is quite addicting, and with good reason—it was designed to hold fast the unbidden minds that drifted into it, whether intentionally or otherwise. It is a veil meant to be so glamorous that the mere access of it immediately conjures illusions of ascension and enlightenment that are not yet truly manifest. The elation of initially breaking free of the physical chains can bring such ecstasy that the naïve neophyte actually believes they "have arrived," when really they have just begun. As the enigmatic editor Simon warns—

> "It is the initiatory plane, and it is here, at the Lunar Gate, that the vast majority of occultists lose their way, forever. For most people, it is the repository of every inspirational, delusional, ghostly, spiritual, hallucinogenic event that has ever transpired in their lives. The temptation of this plane is to become one of those vague, ethereal types one finds spouting psychobabble on morning talk shows. Many channelers are victims of staying too long on the Lunar level; astral puppets who never progress beyond sitting on the ventriloquist's lap... instead of mastering this plane, it has become *their* master; every breeze that brushes across their faces become a caress from beyond, every news item a direct message from an entity on Alpha Centauri. Avoid them like the very plague..."

The astral "shade-forms" of NANNA-SIN and NINGAL reflect an archetypal otherworldly "fairy" king and queen—born of heaven, ruling on earth and embodied in the lunar threshold connecting between the two. Most mystics encountering these personas have seen them in their elderly form, but the blue-hued moonlight radiating from their skin gives off so much beauty that we tend to think of them as ageless. The color associated with the moon is silver and the essence and symbol attributed to NANNA is the royal wand or scepter of lapis lazuli.

When the moon was not visible, it was thought to be dwelling in the underworld. When a lunar eclipse occurred, Sumerian tradition described the moon battling wicked demons before reappearing. This more active face of the lunar current is not often tapped by most "magical" tables of correspondence. We can find similar beliefs concerning the disappearance-and-appearance of the *Sun* and *Moon* throughout mythologies of many ancient cultures. The Mardukite "Invocation of the Nanna Gate" given in *"Necronomicon: The Anunnaki Bible"* very closely resembles an incantation found from the tablet-series known to scholars as: "Prayers of the Lifting of the Hand."—the entire basis for L.W. King's *"Babylonian Magic & Sorcery."* The original prayer is as follows—

> O SIN! O NANNAR! Mighty One . . . [among the gods]
> *siptu ilu-SIN ilu-NANNARU ru-su-bu u-* . . .
>
> O SIN, who art unique, thou that brightens . . . [the heavens]
> *ilu-SIN id-dis-su-u, mu-nam-mir* . . .
>
> That gives light unto the nations . . . [over the four lands]
> *sa-ki-in na-mir-ti a-na nisi-* . . .
>
> That unto the black-headed race art favorable . . . [god to your people]
> *ana nisi sal-mat kakkadu us-su-ru sa-* . . .
>
> Bright is thy light, in heaven . . . [like fire]
> *nam-rat urru-ka ina sami-i* . . .
>
> Brilliant is thy torch, like the fire-god . . . [burning brightly]
> *sar-hat di-pa-ra-ka, kima ilu-GIBIL* . . .
>
> Thy brightness fills the broad earth!
> *ma-lu-u nam-ri-ru-ka irsita(ta) rapasta*
>
> The brightness of the nations he gathers, in thy sight . . .
> *sar-ha nisi uk-ta-sa-ra ana a-ma-ri-ka*
>
> O ANU of the sky, whose purpose no man learns!
> *ilu-A-nim sami-i sa la i-lam-ma-du mi-lik-su ma-*
>
> Overwhelming is thy light like the Sun-god, thy first born!
> *su-tu-rat urru-ka kima ilu-SAMAS bu-uk-ri-*

Before thy face the great gods bow down, the fate of the world is set before thee!
kan-su pani-ka ilani rabuti purus matati sakin(in) ina pani-ka

In the evil of an eclipse of the Moon which in X month on X day, has taken place,
ina lumin ilu-atali ilu-SIN sa ina arhi pulani umi pulani isakna(na)

In the evil of the powers, of the portents not good, which are in my palace and my land,
lumun idati iti.mis limniti la tabati sa ina ikalli-ya u mati-ya ibasa-a

The great gods beseech thee and thou gives counsel!
ilani rabuti i-sal-lu-ka-ma tanadin(in) mil-ka

They take their stand, all of them, they petition at thy feet!
izzizu pu-hur-su-nu us-ta-mu-u ina sapli-ka

O SIN, glorious one of IKUR! They beseech you and you give the oracle of the gods!
ilu-SIN su-pu-u sa I.KUR i-sal-lu-ka-ma ta-mit ilani tanadin(in)

The end of the month is the day of thy oracle, the decision of the great gods;
bubbulum u-um ta-mit-ti-ka pi-ris-ti ilani rabuti

The thirtieth day is thy festival, a day of prayer to thy divinity!
umu XXX-kan i-sin-na-ka u-um ta-sil-ti ilu-ti-[ka]

O God of the New Moon, in might unrivaled whose purpose no man learns,
ilu-Namrasit i-muk la sa-na-an sa la i-lam-ma-du mi-lik-su ma- . . .

I have poured thee a libation of the night (with) wailing, I have offered thee (with) shouts of joy a drink offering of . . . [*type of drink*]
as-ruk-ka si-rik musi lallartu ak-ki-ka ri-is-ta-a si-kar . . .

I am bowed down! I have taken my stand! I have sought for thee!
kan-sa-ku az-za-az a-si-ka ka- . . .

Do thou set favor and righteousness upon me!
ka-sa dum-ki u mi-sa-ri sukun(un) ili-[ya]

May my god and my goddess, who for long have been angry with me,
ili-ya u ilu-istari sa is-tu u-um ma-du-ti is-bu-su

In righteousness and justice deal graciously with me! Let my way be favorable, with joy ...
ina kit-ti u misari lis-li-mu itti-ya ur-hi lid-mi-ik had-is ni- ...

And ZA.GAR, the god of dreams hath sent,
u-ma-'-ir-ma ilu-ZA.GAR ilu sa sunati

In the night season ... [cleanse me of] my sin, my iniquity may ... [it be absolved]
ina sat musi Kab.mis ar-ni-ya lu-us-mi sir-ti lu-ta

For ever may I bow myself in humility before thee!
ana da-ra-ti lud-lul da-li-li-[ka]

— 2 —
: NABU-TUTU :
MERCURY – "WHO SPEAKS FOR"

Mythologists and mythographers often associate the Sumerian "Lord of the Tree of Life" [*Ningishzidda*] with the Egyptian deity THOTH—the archetypal Mercurial current shared by Hermes, Merlyn, Ogmios, &tc., but the most iconic *Anunnaki* "messenger of the gods" more appropriately corresponds to a more "Mardukite" character in Babylon. If one carefully considers the "divine" occupation of this lineage in Egypt, there is evidence for a "third party" of gods, apart from strict ENLIL and ENKI lineages, that most strongly influenced the Babylonian system in preference over the former Sumerian one.

In the Babylonian tradition, the "Apollonian herald of the mercurial current" among the "younger pantheon" is the *heir-son* of MARDUK and SARPANIT —the patrons of *Babylon*. This role is attributed to NABU—also *Nebo* or *Nabak* in Semitic language—meaning "spokes-person." He shares residence at the temple-ziggurat of the city of *Borsippa* [*Birs-i-Nimrud*] (approximately ten miles from *Babylon*) with his consort, TASMIT—*Teshmet(um)* or *Tashmitu*. In addition to managing the national school and temple of scribe-priests, NABU and TESMITU made annual visits to *Babylon* for the celebration of the "New Year" [A.KI.TI/Akitu] festival held on the spring equinox.

NABU is the original "scribe of the gods," a patron deity of wisdom-knowledge and writing, inventor of the "reed-stylus" (*pen*), and the first truly refined form of cuneiform—distinguishing the stylus-script of *Babylon* from early pictograms of *Sumer*. His energetic current carries an affinity to Mercury—communication, divination and the air element. Semitic-Hebrew language incorporated the word *"Nabih,"* meaning "prophet." NABU is effectively the "Prophet of MARDUK" and a "Messianic Son" for Mardukites of *Babylon*. Priests and kings evoked his name in the consecration of their libraries, asking him to bless their hands when writing tablets and also to curse those who might steal or desecrate the libraries. The intellectual nature of NABU and his unusual manner of psychological warfare are echoed on an ancient basalt tablet called the *"Caillou Michaux,"* named for the archaeologist excavating it for the French National Museum—

> *May Nebo, the supreme intelligence,*
> *overwhelm him with affliction and terror,*
> *and lastly may he hurry him into incurable despair.*

When the ancient Mardukites were losing ground to the Enlilite-Yahwists during the "Old Testament" biblical era, NABU was charged with the task of maintaining a tradition of MARDUK's followers near *Babylon* and in *Egypt*. Several neo-Babylonian Kings of the time period are also given related names in patronage and reverence to the younger pantheon of the Mardukites, such as: Nabuna'id (*"Nabu is exalted"*), Nabupolassar (*"Nabu protects his son"*) and, of course, Nebochadnezzar (*"Nabu preserve my first-born son"*), just to name a few. For the Mardukites, NABU represented a "messianic prophet"—born of a "Heavenly King" (MARDUK) and ENKI's special hybrid offspring (SARPANIT), long before Semitic and Christian lore existed to record such things, but undoubtedly served as a source of inspiration to later traditions.

Although an old soul—a steward of all wisdom of the gods, responsible for recording their "movements" in a Mesopotamian version of the "Book of Life" called the "Tablets of Destiny"—NABU is actually a relatively young "deity"of the Mardukite Anunnaki pantheon. His other epithet—TU.TU—appears notably as the thirteenth name of the *"Enuma Elis"* (on *Tablet-F* of *"Necronomicon: The Anunnaki Bible"*) that MARDUK assumed during the *"Epic of Creation."* The "name" of this "power" is transferred to NABU in the Babylonian Mardukite Tradition, although the governing domain is quite ambiguous:

> NABU-TUTU,
> *He who created them anew,*
> *And should their wants be pure,*
> *Then they are satisfied.*

This intellectual riddle described the very function NABU serves—the recording of life, history, people... and *gods*—the "eye-of-the-beholder" concerning descendants of the Anunnaki, origins of humanity and courses of life and existence—were now NABU's to hold. He could create them anew, give anyone a new face and past and therefore future. He was the *"Voice of God"*—the "Metatron"—the messenger frequency of the highest brought to the lowest and an intermediary between.

Mesopotamian religion held a firm inseparable view of male-female aspects in divinity, but the relationship between NABU and TASMIT is truly complimentary—where NABU is a projector of communication, TASMIT is a receiver. She is the Babylonian "goddess of hearing," the one who listens to the prayers—often sought as a *"transmit"* to her husband and the other deities. A powerful incantation to *"Tesmitu"* is found on the reverse-side of the prayer-tablet referenced previously for NANNA.

The incantation is specifically a petition to "remove sickness and enchantments caused by an eclipse of the Moon"—

> O Lady TASMITU!
> I __ , son of ___ and ___ ,
> Whose god is ___ , whose goddess is ___ ,
> In the evil of an eclipse of the Moon,
> Which in ___ month on ___ day has taken place,
> In the evil of the powers, of the portents,
> Evil and not good, which are in my palace and my land,
> I have turned towards thee!
> I have established thee!
> Listen to the incantation!
> Before NABU thy spouse, the lord, the prince,
> The firstborn son of E.SAGILA, intercede for me!
> May he hearken to my cry at the word of thy mouth;
> May he remove my sighing;
> May he learn of my supplication!
> At his mighty word,
> May god and goddess deal graciously with me!
> May the sickness of my body be torn away;
> May the groaning of my flesh be consumed!
> May the consumption of my muscles be removed!
> May the poisons that are upon me be loosened!
> May the ban be torn away and the curse consumed!
> May the Anunnaki come forth and demand justice!
> At thy command, may mercy be established!
> May god and king ordain favor
> At thy mighty command that is not altered,
> And thy true mercy that changes not,
> O Lady TASMITU!

* * *

Perhaps one of the most fundamental lessons to be learned via the mercurial current is *discernment*. Once the veils have been penetrated and the spectral showers of vast images and illusions are tapped on the lunar level, *temperance* is required. Where the *Moon Gate* provides access to the "magical path," the *Mercury Gate* (*"Nabu Gate"*) is the beginning of the "mystical path," concerning the "Secret Doctrines of the Cosmos" contained on the "Tablets of Destiny." The half-truths of worldly glamours must be stripped away. True knowledge must replace all misinformation.

Our intellect causes psychosomatic effects on our emotional state, which in turn influences our behavior. The methodology suggested taps undefiled unconditioned stimuli from beyond the veil of tangible experiential based memory data. This ensures a higher rate of success generating transcendental moments of *"true gnosis,"* and not merely trivial enlightenment-delusions of false-light. The *light on the screen* can be made to be seen for what it is.

The "weight of wisdom" often causes NABU to appear relatively much older than he actually is. His number is twelve, a fundamental value to the *"sexagesimal"* (Base-60) mathematics of Mesopotamia, a method still used today to denote time, angles, locales and speed of travel across any space. His traditional color is blue, and in addition to the "stylus," NABU is represented by the double-barred cross, also visible in his cuneiform sign. The usual Mardukite invocation made to NABU (in *"Necronomicon: The Anunnaki Bible"*) resonates strongly with the twenty-second prayer of the *"Lifting of the Hand"* cuneiform tablet series—

> O hero, prince, first-born of MARDUK!
> *siptu rubu asaridu bu-kur ilu-MARDUK*
>
> O prudent ruler, offspring of ZARPANITU!
> *Massu-u i-ti-ip-su i-lit-ti ilu-ZARPANITU*
>
> O NABU, bearer of the Tablet of Destiny of the gods, Director of E.SAGILA!
> *Ilu-NABU na-as duppu si-mat ilani a-sir E.SAG.ILA*
>
> Lord of E.ZIDA, Shadow of Borsippa,
> *bil E.ZID.DA su-lul duru-BORSIPPA-ki*
>
> Darling of IA [ENKI], Giver of Life,
> *na-ram ilu-IA ka-i-su balatu*
>
> Prince of Babylon, Protector of the Living,
> *asarid BAB.ILI na-si-ru na-pis-ti*
>
> Lofty Lord of the hill-dwelling, fortress of the nations, Lord of temples!
> *ilu du-ul da-ad-mi kar misi bil is-ri-ti*
>
> Thy name is the word in the mouth of the people, O sedu ["spirit"]
> *zi-kir-ka ina pi nisi su.dub.ba ilu-sidu*

O son of the mighty prince MARDUK, in thy mouth is justice!
mar rubi rabi ilu-MARDUK ina pi-ka kit-ti

In thy illustrious name, at the command of thy mighty godhead,
ina si-ik-ri-ka kabti ina ki-bit ilu-ti-ka rabiti(ti)

I ___ , the son of ___ and ___ , who am smitten with disease, thy servant,
ana-ku pulanu apil pulani mar-su sum-ru-su arad-ka

Whom the hand of the demon and breath of the wicked [spirit has seized],
sa kat utukki-ma imat bur.ru.da nam-kil-lu-ni-ma nal-susu-ni

May I live, may I be perfect [with your wisdom]
lu-ub-lut lu-us-lim-ma . . . gub.bu.du luksud(ud)

Set justice in my mouth!
su-us-kin kit-ti ina pi-ya

[Kindle] mercy in my heart!
sup-si-ka damikti(ti) ina libbi-ya

May the Anunnaki return and be established! May they command mercy!
ti-i-ru u an.nu.na.ki man-za-[za lik-bu-u] damikti(ti)

May my god stand at my right hand!
li-iz-ziz [ili-ya] ina imni-ya

May my goddess stand at my left hand!
li-iz-ziz [ilu-istari-ya] ina sumili-ya

May the favorable sidu [spirit], the favorable lamassu [guardian] be with me!
ilu-sidu damiktu ilu-lamassu damiktu . . . -kis illi-ya

— 3 —
: INANNA-ISHTAR :
VENUS – "QUEEN OF HEAVEN"

Known in *Egypt* as "Goddess of Ten-Thousand Names," a unique position of *"Queenship of Heaven"* is reserved by one of the "younger pantheon" in both Sumerian and later Chaldeo-Babylonian systems. Daughter of NANNA and NINGAL—the Sumerian aspects of the Moon—and twin to SHAMMASH (the Sun), this title of high esteem is passed on to a young "Lady of the Stars"—unequaled in beauty and cunning use of divine politics. In ancient Sumer, she is introduced in the original cuneiform literature as IN.ANNA —"Lady of ANU" and *"Queen of Heaven."*

INANNA quickly rises in status as the "archetypal goddess" on earth. She simultaneously represents both a "goddess of love" and "goddess of war," granting her significant domain in the physical world. As a result, she was favored among the masses adoring her for her influence. She is originally given a numeric designation of 5 in Sumer—but in Mardukite Babylon she receives 15, replacing the position held by NINMAH (*Ninhursag*) from the elder pantheon. She remains a primary goddess in Assyro-Babylonian tradition, with the name I.STAR (or *Ishtar*)—"The Goddess"—*istari* being the Akkadian word for "goddess." Her traditional/ceremonial color is sometimes white (INANNA) and sometimes light-green (*Venus*).

Assyrian art frequently depicts INANNA-ISHTAR with wings. The same winged form is visible on her Egyptian form as ISIS. Clearly she was a goddess of the aerial world, not only the *"Anunit-(um)"* ("ANU's Beloved"), but literally a "queen" of the skies, stars or heavens. Mythological cycles describe seven objects connected to ISHTAR for her aerial travels. Similarly, there are seven garments and ornaments removed during her "Descent to the Underworld." It is quite likely that these items are related to her position as "Lady of the Stars" or "Queen of Heaven"—power symbols associated with this role. Mystical revivalists consider this symbolism significant for modern ritual magic activities reviving Mesopotamian-based ceremonialism (and the Underworld), but perhaps they have an even greater unseen esoteric relevance. In the cuneiform tablet account of ISHTAR's "Crossings to the Underworld" (given as *Tablet-C* in *"Necronomicon: The Anunnaki Bible"*), these objects are referred to as seven "Divine Decrees" that she "fixes" to her body. They are listed as—

1. Shugurra – Starry Crown of Anu (on her head)
2. Wand of Lapis Lazuli (in her hand)
3. Necklace of Lapis Lazuli (around her neck)
4. Bag of Brilliant-Shinning-Stones (carried)
5. Gold Ring of Power (on her finger)
6. Frontlet Amulet (as a breastplate)
7. The Pala – Royal Garments (worn about her body)

Zecharia Sitchin interprets the talismans differently, describing "Seven Objects" of INANNA that were "necessary for traveling the skies"—

1. *Shu.gu.ra* – she put on her head
2. Measuring pendents – on her ears
3. Chains of small blue stones – around her neck
4. Twin stones – on her shoulders
5. A golden cylinder – in her hands
6. Straps – clasping her breast
7. *Pa.la* garment – clothed around her body

Genealogies of Sumer detail INANNA as a "fourth generation" Anunnaki figure—daughter of NANNA, born of ENLIL, son of ANU—and is therefore the "great-granddaughter" of ANU. She receives a special place in his heart, which proves beneficial in her rise to power. Even more than this, INANNA is a very actively determined personality that stops at nothing to acquire what she deems rightfully hers. If she wants it, she will take it. In the mythic cycles, this includes "decrees of heaven," "decrees of earth," "secret names of gods" and everything in between. In many ways, her post-Sumerian cult following rivaled MARDUK for supremacy in *Babylon*. She quite effectively used these powers to win an eternal loyalty from mortals in exchange for granting select worldly desires. The kings she favored, she would stand beside in battle and those she did not (or who fell out of favor) she would lend aid to the opposing side, proving that this "goddess of love" is not to be scorned.

The actual truth of how this "archetypal goddess" figure rose to high power is not so widely known. Her many names have, however, become legendary —not only in Mesopotamia as INANNA and ISHTAR, but elsewhere as *Isis*, *Aphrodite*, *Venus*, *Astarte*, *Metis*, *Brigit* (among countless other names)— marking her widespread appearance among many diverse cultures. Later religious misogynists could not recognize such vast power as a female form, transferring her identity to *Ashtoreth* or *Astoroth*—a leader of a demonic hierarchy of angels in the Judeo-Christian Semitic and Kabbalistic systems.

The original Sumerian tablet cycle involving INANNA and ENKI is academically called *"The Transfer of the Arts of Civilization from Eridu to Erech."* Seeking greater abundance and power for her city, INANNA travels to *Eridu*—the residence of ENKI—in pursuit of secret knowledge, holy relics and tablets of power that will enable her to achieve this. Her charm, coupled with the looseness that comes with heavy drinking, won over ENKI, who gave up some one-hundred decrees and treasures in his compromised state. These are then loaded onto her "Boat of Heaven" and transported back to *Erech*, intermittently making seven rest stops along the way. Having realized what he's done soon after, ENKI immediately sends his counselor ISIMUD with a host of monsters in pursuit of ISHTAR, but the damage is done and she arrives safely in *Erech* with her new found "decrees" intact. We might compare this account to the acquisition of power by ISIS in *Egypt*, as deTraci Regula describes—

> "Her skill as a magician was employed when she sought to receive the sacred true name of Ra, her father in some stories. Ra was ignoring the needs of humanity and Isis resorted to a drastic act of magic, creating a small snake from the exudation of his body, which bit him. To stop the pain, Ra agreed to give Isis his most secret name, allowing her to restore balance."

A romantic patina for INANNA-ISHTAR is toned by the Romeo-and-Juliet-motif in the relationship with her consort—DAMUZI (*Dumuzi*) [Sumerian; *"the good son"*] or in Babylon, TAMMUZ *"the good shepherd."* There are many different accounts of their courtship activities and later involvement with the Underworld. [See *Tablet-U* from *"Necronomicon: The Anunnaki Bible."*] One version describes how INANNA was head-over-heels overtaken with DAMUZI from the start. However, another tablet series explains that at the beginning, the "shepherd-god"—DAMUZI—is rivaling with a "farmer-god" for her love and affections. Not surprisingly, DAMUZI is the youngest son of ENKI, and apart from MARDUK, NABU and few others, he was an "officially" acceptable spouse in the tradition of Anunnaki "succession." This was later maintained among the "younger generation" via a combination of the lineages—in this case, a daughter of ENLIL and a son of ENKI.

INANNA-ISHTAR's rise to power was by no means an arbitrary event. Its significance affected the history of the Anunnaki, but also the evolution of civilization as a whole—the politics, religious beliefs and spiritual traditions. She even maintained high recognition as a patron of Babylon. But it was not the *position* itself that changed the fate of the planet—it was, instead, the *responsibilities* that came with it.

Anunnaki tradition held the "succession" matter as of highest importance for maintaining domain leadership. It became customary for the "younger generation" lineages of ENLIL and ENKI to commingle. For ISHTAR, it was MARDUK—heir of ENKI—that was her intended spouse. Each perfectly complimented one another as the *apex leadership* of the younger pantheon. But, neither party seemed interested in maintaining this obligation as a "team"—so, it never occurred. The role of consort was passed onto ENKI's youngest son, DUMUZI. It initially seemed that everyone agreed to this arrangement, but it resulted in fracturing the powers, creating a third party of gods. The Anunnaki lineage of ENKI *separated*—the followers of MARDUK versus worshipers of ISHTAR throughout *Sumer.*

When MARDUK retreats to *Egypt* to regain supremacy of his own "Mardukite" tradition, ISHTAR sets her sights on making the powers *there* her own as well. We can certainly see evidence for a significant influence that ISIS provides for our contemporary general understanding of *Egypt.* The "fighting" that erupts between "brothers" thereafter may be of a similar theme to what is alluded in the "farmer-god versus shepherd-god" stories (concerning ISHTAR's courtship of a mate). ISHTAR's "undying love" for DUMUZI is explicitly expressed. Quarreling among the family reaches climactic heights when DUMUZI drowns under uncertain circumstances. It is then that ISHTAR marches on MARDUK (known as "Ra" there, to the Egyptians), arriving with the Horus-Seth tribes—fracturing the pantheon in Egypt too, as Zecharia Sitchin explains:

> "The first presence of Inanna/Ishtar in Egypt is mentioned in the Edfu text dealing with the First Pyramid War. Called there Ashtoreth (her Canaanite name), she is said to have appeared on the battlefield among the advancing forces of Horus. . . as long as the fighting was only between the descendants of Enki, no one saw a particular problem in having a granddaughter of Enlil around. But after the victory of Horus, when Seth occupied lands not his, the situation changed completely: the Second Pyramid War pitched the sons and grandchildren of Enlil against the descendants of Enki."

* * *

Mystical experiences with INANNA-ISHTAR's *Venusian* energy current are prevalent throughout the ages across nearly all ancient cultures. She is favored by priests and priestesses of many esoteric and occult traditions many times over for thousands of years.

As a self-made "goddess queen" of the *Heavens* and the material domains—love, lust, war, magic—her coveted position of influence is unparalleled among the pantheon. It becomes clear why her intended betrothed was MARDUK, but as they rivaled for the same side of the same coin, they really became the same side of two coins.

Although Mesopotamian literature provides a wide array of Anunnaki activity, the colorful picture portrayed in the original system is *"amoral"* or concerns a *"higher ethic"* than readily discernible in mortal life. In fact, this *"utilitarian"* ideal, for better or worse, is demonstrated by most any "higher order" of "authority," which is often mysterious to those it governed. In some form—physically and in memory—the "younger pantheon" of Anunnaki were the "gods" of earth religions for thousands of years, even preferred (in contrast to their elders) for their worldly material accessibility.

As Guardian of the *Venus Gate*, INANNA-ISHTAR is encountered on the mystic path as a moral challenge to rise above the pleasures of earth and seek a higher spiritual gratification. Should the initiate succumb to these temptations she will undoubtedly reward such as well, but there is a strict clause to such attainment that is well known to occultists—

> *Inanna-Ishtar takes her own for her own,*
> *And that once chosen by her,*
> *No man may take another bride.*

There are no shortages of Babylonian tablets revealing prayers, rites and incantations in honor of ISHTAR. Her allied tradition in *Babylon* consists of the same offerings that priests and priestesses offered MARDUK—the sprinkling of pure waters, libations and potent beverages, fragrant oils, honey and butter with bread, with sacred woods burning as incense. The number *"seven"* frequently appears in these ancient ceremonies—it was often customary to present a food or drink offering seven times. Or, in other instances, such as the *"pure waters,"* offerings are sprinkled about the ground. Other times, vials and jars were left at an *"Altar of Offerings"* dedicated to a specific deity. Once the gods physically left, people on earth retained only memories of their existence, but the temple-priests (and their families) were continuously sustained thereafter, living on the offerings that once supported the physical existence of great Anunnaki figures.

Like the other examples, invocation-prayers to ISHTAR used by modern Mardukites are similar to those found on the *"Prayers of the Lifting of the Hand"* tablet-series from the Kuyunjik collection—

O ISHTAR, good is thy supplication, when the spirit of thy name is propitious [favorable/powerful].
[ilu-ISTAR] ta-a-bu su-up-pu-u-ki ki-i ki-ru-ub nis sumi-ki

Thy regard is prosperity, thy command is light!
[nap]-lu-us-ki tas-mu-u ki-bit-ki nu-u-ra

Have mercy on me, O ISHTAR! Command abundance!
rimi-nin-ni-ma ilu-ISTAR ki-bi-i na-ha-si

Truly pity me and take away my sighing.
ki-nis nap-li-si-in-ni-ma li-ki-i un-ni-ni-ya

. . . .
ir-di uz-ki is-di-hu li- . . .

Thy [feet or hands(?)] have I held: let me bring joy of heart!
sar-ta-a-ki a-hu-zu lu-bi-il tu-ub libbi- . . .

I have borne thy yoke: do thou give [me] consolation!
u-bil ap-sa-na-ki pa-sa-ha suk- . . .

I have [held] thy head: let me enjoy success and favor!
u-ki-' kakkadu-ki li-si-ra sa-li-mu

I have protected thy splendor: let there be good fortune and prosperity!
as-sur sa-ru-ra-ki lu-u tas-mu-u u ma-ga-ru

I have sought thy light: let my brightness shine!
is-ti-'-u nam-[ri]-ir-ri-ki lim-mi-ru zi-mu-u-a

I have turned towards thy power: let there be life and peace!
as-hur bi-lut-ki [lu]-u balatu u sul-mu

Propitious be the favorable spirit who is before thee: may the *lamassu* that goes behind thee be propitious!
lu tas-lim ilu-sidu damiktu sa pa-ni-ki sa ar-ki-ki a-li-kat ilu-lammasu lu tas-lim

That which is on thy right hand, increase good fortune: that which on thy left hand, attain favor!

> *sa im-nu-uk-ki mis-ra-a lu-us-sip dum-ka lu-uk-su-da sa su-mi-lu-*
> *[uk-ki]*

Speak and let the word be heard!
ki-bi-ma lis-si-mi zik-ri

Let the word I speak, when [spoken], be propitious!
a-mat a-kab-bu-u ki-ma a-kab-bu-u lu-u ma-ag-rat

Let health of body and joy of heart be my daily portion!
ina tu-ub siri u hu-ud lib-bi i-tar-ri-in-ni u-mi-sam

My days prolong, life bestow: let me live, let me be perfect, let me behold thy divinity!
umi-ya ur-ri-ki ba-la-ta surki lu-ub-lut lu-us-lim-ma lu-us-tam-mar ilu-[ut-ki]

When I plan, let me attain (my purpose): Heaven be thy joy, may the Abyss hail thee!
i-ma u-sa-am-ma-ru lu-uk-su-ud samu-u hidutu-ki apsu li-ris-[ki]

May the gods of the world be favorable to thee: may the great gods delight thy heart!
ilani sa kis-sa-ti lik-ru-bu-ki ilani rabuti lib-ba-ki li-tib-[bu]

— 4 —
: SHAMMASH :
THE SUN – "SHINNING ONE"

Ancient Mesopotamian astronomers correctly depicted the *Sun* in the middle-center of the *"Ladder of Lights"*—a stream of energies connecting our physical world to the ALL via a *"bridge,"* often represented by "Celestial Bodies." Assuming the esoteric chronology that begins with the *"Earth Gate,"* the Seeker approaches Gates of local planetary systems—those relatively closer to the Earth: the *Moon*, *Mercury* and *Venus*—and then the *Sun*. According to Sumerian cosmology (and lineage tablets), the *Sun*—or more accurately, the *"sun-god"*—was a twin brother to INANNA-ISHTAR (*Venus*), the "Morning Star" born of NANNA (*the Moon*). This general course also follows with a worldview that "day was born from night" and more esoterically that "light emerges to penetrate the darkness."

The role of the *"sun-god"* as the physical and spiritual "illuminator" carried the very name given to the "face of the sun"—the Anunnaki sky-commander UTU or UDDU (Sumerian for *"shinning one"*). The same appears on cuneiform tablets in Akkadian and Chaldeo-Babylonian languages as SAMAS—often written as it is pronounced: "SHAMMASH"—and *"Babbar"* in some sources. His consort is AYA or AIA (also *"Shendira"*)—from the Akkadian for *"dawn."* Together they shared a sanctuary at *Larsa* (in Sumer); and also a temple in *Sippar* (near Babylon), where the couple eventually retired. SHAMMASH is given the Anunnaki designation of "20" and reign of the solar domain—the task of maintaining order as chief of the Anunnaki "Judges"—governing justice, law, balance and truth. [In fact, the *"Shammash"* title was used by Medieval Jewish communities to designate a person that assisted in maintaining a governing order. The name was even used later to designate a "temple servant."]

SHAMMASH—and the *Sun*—are called forth frequently with incantations from mystical and religious cuneiform tablets from the *Ancient Near East*. However, as a subordinate to many other entities in the pantheon, the system as a whole can hardly be considered "sun-worship" in the conventional sense. It might be more accurately described as "stellar-worship"—if we are even to ascribe the misunderstood word "worship" at all—as all primary *"Olympian"* deities of this tradition were either named for celestial objects, or we must assume they named the planets after themselves.

We can be sure, however, that the *Sun* played a significant role in the "order" of the material world—a "conqueror of evil" (considered sleeping or battling demons at night) or the "protector of travelers" by day, ceaselessly keeping watch over man's daily activities and work-life. The *Sun* clearly became a popular force for the masses to call on, as Lenormant describes—

> "The sun was not one of the highest gods of the religious system which had served as a foundation for Accadian magic, his power did not approach that of the three great spirits of the zones of the universe [governed by the Supernal Trinity]. But it was just his lower rank that made him more accessible to the prayers of man; and the fact that his influence upon man and the phenomena of life was so sensibly felt, made them assign to him the office of arbiter of events and of fate; while lastly, as he dissipated darkness, and consequently was engaged in a struggle with the bad spirits, he became one of the supernatural personages to whom the magical invocations were most frequently addressed."

* * *

The *"Sun Gate"* is a significant threshold "crossing" on the mystic path. Many do not reach this far in their spiritual evolution (or "ascension process"). Many are too enamored by trappings of lower realms to reach (and survive) the self-annihilation prominent at this Gate. This veil is bright and shinning—it will surely illuminate any "darkness" within you that is still waiting to be purged, in addition to any other physical and sensation-based delights remaining from the Venusian initiation.

In the Egyptian mythic cycle associated with the *Sun*—Yes, there is "Ra," actually a representative of a *"sun behind the sun"* (even more than our local sun), but more important to our topic is the "Osirian mythos" of death and transformation—the "solar-judge" weighing the soul to measure impurity. The initiate must allow the pictures and images of their "former" programmed existence to be burned away—allow the baggage and energetic attachments of a "lower life" to be dissolved.

> *"I come in self-annihilation and the grandeur of inspiration."*
> – William Blake

The challenge-riddle of the *"Sun Gate"* is: "all that glitters is not gold." Just as surely as the sunlight can pierce the darkness, so too is it sometimes blinding to see what is right in front of us. We must be ready, always, not caught basking in the glowing rays of the shining sun. The apex of solar power at noon reflects the heights of empires and all systems—but these too must ebb and fall in their own cyclic tides. Everything is in motion; and everything everywhere is connected together.

It is from the *"Solar Gate"* that an initiate must prepare in "self-honesty" for the forthcoming encounter with the "Annihilator" energies of NERGAL. After being given charged on the Mardukite mystic path of the *"Ladder of Lights"* by NABU at the second gate, there are many Anunnaki figures (representing lessons on the path) from those who stood against the rise of a *Mardukite Babylon*—ISHTAR, SHAMMASH and NERGAL—all of which have played a part in its abolition. Even SHAMMASH (UTU) sided with DUMUZI against MARDUK in that tablet cycle; and then later against NABU, siding with NERGAL and NINURTA in what some scholars call the "Pyramid Wars," which resulted in mass-destruction of the ancient "Middle East," leaving a resonant imprint of unrest forever on that locale.

"The Great Hymn of Shammash" is potentially the most significant mystical cuneiform tablet transcription from Mesopotamia regarding the *"sun-god."* A seeker will see that it reveres more than simply the "physical *sun*," but the "sublime light of truth" personified by the Anunnaki position held SHAMMASH (UTU). Several of the lines (particularly at the beginning and end) on the tablet cycle have worn away, but the definitive academic version, first appearing in *"Babylonian Wisdom Literature"* by W. Lambert (in 1960), remains the most complete modern translation for both mystics and scholars. The "dogma" presented reflects other Babylonian wisdom tablets, such as the "Book of the Law of Marduk" given as the *Tablet-L* series in *"Necronomicon: The Anunnaki Bible."* The hymn reads—

    21. You climb to the mountains surveying the earth,
    22. You suspend from the heavens the circle of the lands,
    23. You care for all the peoples of the lands,
    24. And everything that EA (ENKI), king of the counselors had created is entrusted to you.
    25. Whatever has breath you shepherd without exception,
    26. You are keeper in upper and lower regions.
    27. Regularly and without cease you traverse the heavens,
    28. Every day you pass over the broad earth . . .
    33. Shepherd of that beneath, keeper of that above,
    34. You, SHAMMASH, direct, you are the light of everything.

35. You never fail to cross the wide expanse of sea,
36. The depth of which the IGIGI know not.
37. SHAMMASH, your glare reaches down to the abyss
38. So that monsters of the deep behold your light . . .
45. Among all the IGIGI there is none who toils but you,
46. None who is supreme like you in the whole pantheon of gods.
47. At your rising the gods of the land assemble,
48. Your fierce glare covers the land.
49. Of all the lands of varied speech,
50. You know their plans, you scan their way.
51. The whole of mankind bows to you,
52. SHAMMASH, the universe longs for your light.
88. A man who covets his neighbor's wife
89. Will . . . before his appointed day.
90. A nasty snare is prepared for him . . .
91. Your weapon will strike at him, and there will be none to save him.
92. His father will not stand for his defense,
93. And at the judge's command his brothers will not plead.
94. He will be caught in a copper trap that he did not foresee.
95. You destroy the horns of a scheming villain,
96. A zealous . . . his foundations are undermined.
97. You give the unscrupulous judge experience fetters,
98. Him who accepts a present and yet lets justice miscarry, you make bear his punishment.
99. As for him who declines a present but nevertheless takes the part of the weak,
100. It is pleasing to SHAMMASH, and he will prolong his life . . .
124. The progeny of evil-doers will fail.
125. Those whose mouth says "No," their case is before you.
126. In a moment you discern what they say;
127. You hear and examine them; you determine the lawsuit of the wronged.
128. Every single person is entrusted to your hands;
129. You manage their omens; that which is perplexing you make plain.
130. You observe, SHAMMASH, prayer, supplication, and benediction,
131. Obeisance, kneeling, ritual murmurs, and prostration.
132. The feeble man calls you from the hollow of his mouth,
133. The humble, the weak, the afflicted, the poor,
134. She whose son is captive constantly and unceasingly confronts you.

135. He whose family is remote, whose city is distant,
136. The shepherd amid the terror of the steppe confronts you,
137. The herdsman in warfare, the keeper of sheep among enemies.
138. SHAMMASH, there confronts you the caravan, those journeying in fear,
139. The traveling merchant, the agent who is carrying capital.
140. SHAMMASH there confronts you the fisherman with his net,
141. The hunter, the bowman who drives the game,
142. With his bird net the fowler confronts you.
143. The prowling thief, the enemy of SHAMMASH,
144. The marauder along the tracks of the steppe confronts you.
145. The roving dead, the vagrant soul,
146. They confront you, SHAMMASH, and you hear all.
147. You do not obstruct those that confront you...
148. For my sake, SHAMMASH, do not curse them!
149. You grant revelations, SHAMMASH, to the families of men,
150. Your harsh face and fierce light you give to them...
154. The heavens are not enough as the vessel into which you gaze,
155. The sum of the lands is inadequate as a seer's bowl...
159. You deliver people surrounded by mighty waves,
160. In return you receive their pure, clear libations...
165. They in their reverence laud the mention of you,
166. And worship your majesty for ever...
174. Which are the mountains not clothed with your beams?
175. Which are the regions not warmed by the brightness of your light?
176. Brightener of gloom, Illuminator of darkness,
177. Dispeller of darkness, Illuminator of the broad earth...

Invoking the "solar force"—whether SHAMMASH or by another name—is common not only to the mysticism of Sumer and Babylon, but throughout esoteric history. The name "SAMAS" is called upon no less than a dozen times throughout the "Maqlu" (Maklu) cuneiform tablet series (given as *Tablets–M1-9* in "*Necronomicon: The Anunnaki Bible*"). In many instances from the *Maqlu series*, SHAMMASH is called alongside MARDUK to destroy the wickedness and evil-doers in the world. Although SHAMMASH later sided against MARDUK, the name is invoked in Mardukite literature of the "*Ladder of Lights*" (or "*Stairway to the Stars*"), following the original Babylonian ideal of "unification," even if only to maintain control of the entire Anunnaki pantheon under MARDUK—just as we see with the inclusion of many other Anunnaki names in the Babylonian paradigm. The "Law-Code" attributed to *King Hammurabi*, is dedicated to a "divine" knowledge transmission from both SHAMMASH and MARDUK—

By the command of SAMAS
The Judge of Heaven and Earth,
May truth and righteousness reign supreme
Throughout the lands.
Let those who read these words have a pure heart
And pray to MARDUK, my Lord,
And SARPANIT, my Lady, his consort.
By the decree of SAMAS,
I have been given my Eternal Legacy.
If a forthcoming ruler should read my words
And not corrupt the law,
Then may SAMAS extend the length of his reign on Earth,
And he shall ever reign in righteousness over his subjects.

The mystical incantation of the *"Shammash Gate"* was strongly influenced by the previously given hymn. No prayer dedicated solely to SHAMMASH (or the "sun-god") was found in the *Kuyunjik* collection. Instead, like the *Maqlu* series, the Babylonian invocations in that series are directed to both SAMAS and MARDUK. One interesting example, however, is a badly fractured tablet-incantation from *"Prayers of the Lifting of the Hand"* – *Tablet 53*, to be used "against the evils attending an eclipse of the moon." It is directed to EA (ENKI), SHAMMASH and MARDUK. Leonard King offers the following description of the eclipse tablet—

"No. 53 (*K 3859 + Sm. 383*) preserves the bottom portion of a tablet and contains a prayer to *Ia*, *Samas*, and *Marduk*, of which both the beginning and end are missing. The supplicant states that he is praying after an eclipse of the Moon and he implores these three deities to rescue him from the clutches of a spectre, by whom he is continually haunted. What remains of the *Obverse* commences as follows:—

O arbiter of the world, Marduk, the mighty, the lord of Itura!
abkal kis-sa-ti ilu-Marduk sal-ba-[bu bil] I.TURRA

O EA, Samas, and Marduk deliver me,
ilu-I-a ilu-Samas u ilu-Marduk ya-a-si ru-sa-nim-ma

And through your mercy let me come to prosperity!
ina an-ni-ku-nu i-sa-ru-tu lul-lik

O Samas, the spectre that striketh fear, that for many days
ilu-Samas ikimmu mu-pal-li-hi sa is-tu u-mi ma-'-du-ti

Has been bound on my back, and is not loosed,
  arki-ya rak-su-ma la muppatiru(ru)

Through the whole hath . . . me, through the whole night hath stricken me with terror!
  ina kal u-mi iksus-an-ni ina kal musi up-ta-na-lah-an-ni

The supplicant then describes the ways in which he is tormented by the spectre, who defiles him and attacks his face, his eyes, his back, his flesh and his whole body. On the reverse of the tablet he recounts to *Samas* how he has tried to appease and to restrain his tormentor. Apparently his efforts have met with no success for he now turns to the *Sun-god* for relief, which he prays he may receive through his mighty command that is not altered, and through the command of *Marduk*, the arbiter of the gods."

— 5 —
: NERGAL & ERESHKIGAL :
MARS & THE SHADOWLANDS

The legendary *"Underdark"* or *"Realm of the dead"* has been all too colorfully—or perhaps mono-chromatically—depicted by mythographers as merely a pile a rotting bodies, an infinite swamp, or with the arrival of dualism—a hellfire of intolerable damnation. Cuneiform tablet descriptions of the *"Shadowlands"*—or the "Great Below"—are conceivably "darker" in the spectrum of mortal comprehension. Traversing the Celestial Spheres on the *"Ladder of Lights,"* we are confronted with a "Dweller of the Threshold" to our "Dark Night of the Soul"—and ultimately a spiritual rebirth—rising as a "phoenix"... as a *"god,"* readied for access to the (next) *"Marduk Gate."* Figures of the *"Underworld zonei"* play important functions and roles affecting humanity consciousness regarding death, entropy and physical cycles observed in the cosmos. Any "good" or "bad" is based strictly on human sentiment. The *"Kingdom of Shadows"*—access to its true knowledge and mystical interpretation of these energetic currents—has been shrouded in occult mystery for a very long time, and perhaps for good reason.

Where INANNA-ISHTAR is the *"goddess of love and war"* for the "upper realm," "realm of light (or stars)," and "world of life," her *sister*, ERESHKIGAL was so for the "lower realm," equated with the *"Underworld"* or *"Land of the Dead."* She shares this domain with NERGAL—the "death-god" or "plague-god"—archetypal "war-god" representing the *Martian* energy current. The word "KI.GAL" (as in *"Eresh-Ki-Gal"*) is usually translated by scholars in academia as *"Great Below."* This is a curious ascription when nearly all other cuneiform applications of the word "KI" (for *"Ki-Gal"*) suggest a literal meaning: "Great Earth" or "Great Lands." The position-role and accepted lineage of ERESHKIGAL remains stable across most contemporary interpretations, but such is not the case with NERGAL.

NERGAL—the *"Great Watcher"*—(NER = *"Watcher,"* GAL = *"Great"*) is something of an enigma on tablet sources. Early twentieth century scholars could not ascertain his parentage definitively. More importantly, the designation given to him of "eight" is not harmonious with the Base-60 system of Mesopotamian mathematics—where other Anunnaki designations are divisible by "60"—nor is *Ninib-Adad*, the Babylonian "storm-god" (also within this pantheon) who bares the number "four." This may be appropriate as the two deities are connected in the *Erra Epos* tablet cycle.

However, the fact remains that: given the Sumerian ambiguity left to us from the available cuneiform sources, at best we can assume his father (or grandfather) is either ENLIL or ENKI. We only know for certain that NERGAL is not directly the offspring of ANU. If he were, he would be listed higher in the pantheon. But, NERGAL is too young for this, anyways.

Based on known Anunnaki marriage customs, it would be appropriate if NERGAL were actually the love-child of ENLIL and NINLIL as Kramer describes—

> "*Enlil*, (still) impersonating 'the man of the gate,' cohabits with her [*Ninlil*] and impregnates her. As a result *Ninlil* conceives *Meslamtaea*, more commonly known as *Nergal*."

In contrast, the late controversial Sumeriologist, Zecharia Sitchin, suggests ENKI as NERGAL's father in his genealogical accounts. This might be more plausible, making NERGAL and ERESHKIGAL "half-siblings," in a similar manner found between MARDUK and ISHTAR. In this way, their union—an embodiment of "divine couplehood,"—would have been "blessed" by the Anunnaki Assembly of "gods," much as a union of MARDUK and ISHTAR would have been. It is sometimes confusing because by standards of the "younger pantheon" and Mardukite tradition, ENKI is practically everyone's "*Father*"—the one they all go to regardless of lineage.

ENKI plays a very fatherly for ERESHKIGAL during one of the earliest Sumerian tablet cycles, describing primordial creation—when she is carried off to "*Kutha*" or the "*Underworld*" by the serpent-monster, KUR. Of all the "*Elder Gods*," it is ENKI who goes after her—though she is later made "*Queen of the Underworld*" and allowed to remain there. By this account, ENKI is the first of very few who ever "descend" to the realm of the "dead" and able to return permanently ["*resurrected*"] from that state— the others being ISHTAR and MARDUK—in recorded epics.

Modern traditions observe ERESHKIGAL as an archetypal "*Dragon Queen of the Netherworld*," ruling with her dark king, NERGAL. [Their courtship is described on *Tablet-U* from "*Necronomicon: The Anunnaki Bible*."] In essence, she replaces the KUR-current for Babylon, and she is given domain over the seven Egyptian-Osirian "*death-gates*," fluently described in both Egyptian sources and the INANNA-ISHTAR tablet cycle of "*Descent to the Underworld*." She is given a role of high esteem by the "seven" Anunnaki Judges, encountering every dead spirit to pass through the gates. Egyptologist, E.A. Budge, explains—

> "After the spirit had appeared before *Ereshkigal*, it seems that the *Anunnaki* sat in judgment upon it, and with *Mammitu*, the goddess of the destinies of men, proceeded to discuss the good and evil deeds that it had done in the body."

NERGAL, however, moves back and forth across the *"Underworld Gates"* acting as an *"angel of death"*—the *Ares/Mars* "god of destruction" in the pantheon. The two *"Shadowland"* rulers have quite the collaborative enterprise with one half acting as a "Great Destroyer" and the other half burying the dead. Though not a Christian-like Hell or sickening Hades, the Shadowlands represent the Anunnaki "death-machine" that seals the entire circuit for humanity. The system reveals that the Anunnaki are *Guardians* and *Gatekeepers* of both "Life and Death" for humans in this Earthly material existence.

NERGAL is also known as ENGIDUDU (*"Lord who prowls by night"*)—commander of the *"Sebittu,"* the famous *Seven Demons* of the Anunnaki—used for dealing out plagues and pestilence. But, hardly portrayed as "evil," all of this was originally presented as a means for the gods to maintain "balance." The other Semitic "Angel of Death"—*Azazel*—comes from a "realm of light" or else SHAMMASH, a counterpart of NERGAL in the *Erra Epos*, a tablet cycle describing the Anunnaki politics and destruction of the ancient "Middle East."

As a "war god," NERGAL is invoked for militant blessings in pre-combat rituals. The following Babylonian example from the German anthology, "Ritualtafeln," transcribed by R. Campbell Thomson in *"Semitic Magic"*—

> *Ritual: when an enemy [attacks] the king and his land . . .*
> *The king shall go forth on the right wing of the army,*
> *And thou shalt sweep the earth clean, and sprinkle pure water,*
> *And set [three] altars, one for Ishtar, one for Shammash,*
> *And one for Nergal,*
> *And offer each a loaf of wheaten meal (flour),*
> *And make a mash of honey and butter,*
> *Pouring in dates and . . .-meal,*
> *And sacrifice three full-grown sheep,*
> *Flesh of the right thigh, hinsa-flesh and sume-flesh thou shalt offer*
> *Sprinkle upuntu with cypress on a censer,*
> *And make a libation of honey, butter, wine, oil and scented oil,*
> *Then shalt thou make an image of the foe in tallow,*
> *Bend backwards his face with a cord;*
> *The . . . of the king, who is named like his master,*

Shall . . . the robes of the king . . .
Shall stand before the preparation and repeat this formula before
    Shammash.

NERGAL was never "officially" known as ERRA in Sumer. The *Erra Epos* tablet cycle (also known as *"Erra and Isum"* and given as *Tablet-V* in *"Necronomicon: The Anunnaki Bible"*) is of Akkadian origin. The epithet *"Erra"* is a somewhat derogatory name for NERGAL—a corruption of the names he did possess: *Irrigal* or *Erakal*—with *"Erra"* now meaning a "Servant of Ra" (MARDUK), which he clearly was not. Contemporary translators attribute authorship of this epic to the pen of *Kabti-Ilani-Marduk* —possibly a scribe or priest-king related to a 12th Century B.C. "Babylonian Reformation" under a leader named in the "King Lists" as *Marduk-Kabit-Aheshu*.

The account follows:— MARDUK gives a warning prophecy about the devastation that will ultimately result if he were to step down from his seat at Babylon. This prediction is nothing short of "apocalyptic," describing the ruin of Babylon and all of the great Mesopotamian cities. NERGAL goes to Babylon and explains to MARDUK that his "self-made" supremacy has angered the other (Anunnaki) gods, and that MARDUK is in possession of something (a mysterious object never clearly defined) that not only "powers" or "empowers" Babylon, but all of the other Mesopotamian cities of the gods as well. When MARDUK cannot be convinced to leave "his seat" in Babylon, NERGAL attempts a different tactic by describing various other "holy artifacts" that would ensure his righteous rule. These objects happen to all be in the *"Shadowlands"* and would require retrieval by MARDUK personally. NERGAL promises to "watch over" Babylon while MARDUK is gone and promises very distinctly that nothing will "change" during his absence.

The tablets are obscure about the actual nature of the "holy artifacts" MARDUK goes in search for, or the "object of power" propelling Babylon (kept in a secret room called the *gigunu* that adjoined MARDUK's throne chamber at the top of his ziggurat-temple). But we know that the "object of power" was disturbed by NERGAL as soon as MARDUK "left his seat" in pursuit of the "holy artifacts." Instantly, the "waters stopped flowing," first in Babylon, then in the remaining great cities. The power and strength of ancient Babylon had been weakened, but not yet destroyed. Its destruction came later—a planned attack resulting from mistaken blame for this tragedy, all of which was placed on MARDUK.

When the "Supernal Trinity" called forth the "Anunnaki Assembly" of gods regarding the incident, all of the "younger pantheon"—NINURTA, NERGAL, SHAMMASH, ADAR and ISHTAR—conspired in judgment against MARDUK and NABU, placing full blame on them for the collapse of the systems. Any *unity* of the "celestial pantheon" was split forever.

And with MARDUK absent in pursuit of the "holy artifacts," NABU stood alone to face the entire assembly, as translated by Zecharia Sitchin—

> Speaking for his father, *Nabu* blamed *Ninurta*, and revived the old accusations against *Nergal* in regard to the disappearance of the pre-Diluvial monitoring instruments and the failure to prevent sacrileges in Babylon [referring to the disturbance of the "power object"]; he got into a shouting match with *Nergal*, and showing disrespect:
> *Nabu* to *Enlil*, evil he spoke:
> "There is no justice!
> Destruction was conceived!
> *Enlil* against Babylon caused evil to be planned!"
> It was an unheard of accusation against the Lord of the Command.
> *Enki* spoke up, but it was in defense of his son, not of *Enlil*.
> Asked *Enki*:
> "What are Marduk and Nabu actually accused of?"
> His eye was directed especially at his son *Nergal*:
> "Why do you continue the opposition?"

After the council assembly agrees that MARDUK should be removed from power in Babylon, NERGAL and NINURTA decide to wage an entire nuclear war against Babylon and the "Tribes of NABU." Many lamentation tablets were behind from the wake of this. More devastating than the descriptions of fiery blasts themselves were the accounts of "evil winds" turning entire cities into ghost-towns. Traditions of MARDUK and NABU were moved underground and to *Egypt* where MARDUK already had established a new civilization of followers, presenting himself as "*Amon-Ra*"—"*The Unseen God.*" Devastation in the "Middle East" left its inhabitants and all surrounding-area tribes hostile toward one another—persisting to the present day, a war that has been waging on pointlessly for thousands of years.

* * *

It is easy, then, to understand how NERGAL became the prototype of the *Mars-Ares* personage. As the word *"Erra"* evolved, it later came to denote NERGAL as the "Annihilator," a role previously given in Sumerian literature to GI.BIL—GIRRA or *"fires of god."* NERGAL and SHAMMASH frequently employ these *"fires of god"* to carry out judgments decreed by the Anunnaki Assembly. NERGAL is even described in the *Gilgamesh* cycle as "the ambusher who spares no one." The challenge of the *"Mars Gate"* regarding initiation on Mystical Path is thus the temperance of anger, pride, &tc.—overcoming *all Fear*—destructive energies that will manifest within the initiate uncontrollably chaotic if allowed to pass through the (next) *"Marduk Gate."*

Modern mystical and astral experiences with *"Underworld"* currents reveal these *"Shadowland"* beings as often pale or with blue-hued skin and dark or white hair (sometimes long or unkempt). The absence of clothing also seems prominent in the Underworld, particularly among females. This is best depicted in imagery of the two naked goddesses—ERESHKIGAL and ISHTAR—famously confronting one another in physical rivalry on the floors of the *"Underworld"* palace (in the "Descent" tablet cycle).

The invocation of the *"Nergal Gate"* used by modern Mardukites (as given on *Tablet-B* of *"Necronomicon: The Anunnaki Bible"*) is strongly influenced by the twenty-seventh tablet in the *"Prayers of the Lifting of the Hand"* series from the *Kuyunjik* collection. According to translator, L. W. King, the tablet was originally in possession of *King Ashurbanipal*, so the original inscription bore his name as the benefactor of the prayer's blessings. In this instance, the prayer invokes NERGAL as the first-born of *Nunamnir*, who is ENLIL. The prayer is as follows—

> I mighty lord, hero, first-born of Nunamnir!
> *siptu bi-lum gas-ru ti-iz-ka[ru bu-kur ilu-NU.NAM.NIR]*
>
> Prince of the Anunnaki, lord of the battle!
> *a-sa-rid ilu-A-nun-na-[ki bil tam-ha-ri]*
>
> Offspring of Kutusar, the mighty queen!
> *i-lit-ti ilu-KU.TU.SAR [sar-ra-tum rabitum(tum)]*
>
> O NIRGAL, strong one of the gods, the darling of Ninminna!
> *ilu-Nirgal kas-kas ilani [na-ram ilu-NIN.MIN.NA]*
>
> Thou treadest in the bright heavens, lofty is thy place!
> *su-pa-ta ina sami-i illuti [sa-ku man-za-az-ka]*

Thou art exalted in the Underworld and art the benefactor of its . . .
ra-ba-ta ina aralli-[ma asira(ra) LA.TI-su]

With EA among the multitudes of the gods inscribe thy counsel,
it-ti ilu-I.A. ina puhur [ilani mi-lik-ka su-tur]

With SIN in the heavens, you seek all things,
it-ti ilu-SIN ina sami-i [ta-si gim-ri]

And BIL, thy father has granted thee that the black-headed race, all living creatures,
id-din-ka-ma ilu-BIL abu-[ka sal-mat kakkadu puhur napisti(ti)

The cattle of NIRGAL, created things, thy hand should rule!
bu-ul ilu-NIRGAL nam-mas-[si-i ka-tuk-ka ip-kid]

I, so and so, the son of so and so, am thy servant!
ana-ku pulanu apil pulani [arad-ka]

The . . . of god and goddess are laid upon me!
mi-lat ili u ilu-istari [is-sak-nu-nim-ma]

Uprooting and destruction are my house!
nasahu u hu-lu-uk-ku-[u basu-u ina biti-ya]

[. . .] (untranslated)
ka-bu-u IA si-mu-[u it-tal-pu-nin-ni]

Since thou are beneficent, I have turned to thy divinity!
as-sum gam-ma-la-ta bi-li [as-sa-har ilu-ut-ka]

Since thou are compassionate, I have sought for thee!
as-sum ta-ai-ra-ta [is-ti-'-u-ka]

Since thou are empathic, I have beheld . . .
as-sum mu-up-pal-sa-ta [a-ra-mar . . .]

Since thou are merciful, I have taken my stand before thee!
as-sum ri-mi-ni-ta [at-ta-ziz pani-ka]

Truly pity me and hearken to my cries!
ki-nis naplis-an-ni-ma [si-mi ka-ba-ai]

May thine angry heart have rest!
ag-gu lib-ba-ka [li-nu-ha]

Loosen my sin, my offense . . .
[pu]-tur an-ni hi-[ti-ti . . .]

[. . .] (untranslated / broken)
. . . -sir lib-bi ilu-ti-ka . . .

I god and angry goddess . . .
ilu u ilu-istaru zi-nu-ti sab- . . .

Let me talk of thy greatness, Let me bow in humility before thee!
nir-bi-ka lu-uk-bi [da-li-li-ka lud-lul]

— 6 —
: MARDUK :
JUPITER – KING OF THE GODS

Ancient Mesopotamia witnessed a rise of the "younger pantheon," which took great interest in the activities and devotion of humans on earth. Of them, perhaps the most famous for "planetary mythology" is MARDUK—*Jupiter*—the national god of Babylon. Much like his half-sister—INANNA-ISHTAR—a self-made "queen of the heavens," MARDUK exploited his own personal conviction, cunning and tenacity to secure his position as the primary controller of the *"Ladder of Lights"*—the BAB.ILI, "Gates of the Gods"—even exceeding the position of his father—ENKI—by assuming the role and functions of ENLIL—the ANU of "Material Existence"—to his followers.

Little mention of MARDUK is made in earlier pre-Babylonian Sumerian cuneiform literature. He was content, for a time, to remain an assistant to ENKI, mastering the esoteric arts of "magic" and "science" in *Eridu*. MARDUK was originally given the numeric designation of "10" and told to "wait his turn"—at the *"Age of Aries"*—to rise in the pantheon. His most familiar name—MARDUK—is actually a modern transliteration derived from the Semitic *"meri-dug"* (*Merodach*). An older version of his name is written: AMAR.UTU (*a.mar-utu.ki* = "Light of the Sun on Earth")—often interpreted by contemporary scholars as *"solar calf"* or *"son of the sun."* This provides some background to MARDUK's esteem. And as the foremost son of ENKI, he gained power quickly.

The later Semitic *"Maerdechai"* or *"Mordechai"* came from his name in Chaldeo-Babylonian language—*"silik-mul.u-khi"*—meaning *"Marduk is God."* The more commonly used MAR.DUG means *"son of the pure mound"*—thought to be a reference to pyramids not only in Mesopotamia, but also in Egypt, where he raised himself as the leader of a third party (interpretation) of Anunnaki gods—the Egyptian Pantheon—as *"Amon-Ra,"* again identifying himself with the "solar" current and "stars" directly.

MARDUK's decision to raise himself to a monotheistic-like *"God"* status in Babylon created new political issues for the other Anunnaki on Earth. Exercising his "divine rights" stretched tensions between lineages—of ENKI and ENLIL—for supremacy on earth.

When MARDUK and ISHTAR did not partner for this role, each sought the right to install their own dynastic lineages and choose the humans as "Kings" in their stead), during the "Age of Aries," beginning in 2160 B.C.—the birth of a New Dynastic global era. Zecharia Sitchin explains how in Babylon—

> "*Marduk* was proclaimed King of the Gods, replacing *Enlil*, and the other gods were required to pledge allegiance to him and to come to reside in Babylon where their activities could be easily supervised. This usurpation of Enlilship was accompanied by an extensive Babylonian effort to forge the ancient texts. The most important texts were rewritten and altered so as to make *Marduk* appear as the Lord of the Heavens, the Creator..."

Certainly, the other Anunnaki were less than appreciative of MARDUK's desire to rule over them. Yet throughout the *"Age of Aries,"*—his time to reign —he was not left to his own accord in Babylon (or in Egypt). This seems to have been a disciplinarian act by the other gods. If we take the most literal interpretations at face value, MARDUK lost all rights of kingship "in heaven" when he took a "human" wife instead of his betrothed half-sister. His argument was that his consort—SARPANIT—was a descendent of *Adapa*, and thus of Anunnaki bloodline via ENKI; that ISHTAR was no more interested in the union than he was, and it had not affected her rise to power; and finally, if not "in heaven," why not "on earth"? The logic seems to have gone unheard and where the "Mardukite" legacy was threatened in Babylon and Egypt, as its survival was frequently aided by "foreign hands."

In post-Sumerian Assyrian accounts, MARDUK—as the great "father-god" ASSUR or ASHUR (*"Ashshur"*)—seems to emerge in their tradition as if from nowhere. This led some scholars in the late-1800's and early-1900's to wonder if MARDUK was a purely fictitious figure imagined into being for solely political reasons. Similarly, while SARPANIT—also *Sarapan* or *Zarpanitu*—is mentioned often in Babylonian prayer-tablets, she does not appear in any significant mythic tablet (saga) cycles. Her elevated status is rightly achieved from her direct relationship with MARDUK, and together, they are the parents of NABU. At the spring equinox "A.KI.TI" festival, she is the "spring-maiden" of fertility ceremonies in Babylon. In the *"Edaphic Tradition"* that spread across Europe, she is known as *"Erua,"* or more appropriately, ERU. These later European "elven-faerie-dragon" dynasties claimed descent from MARDUK and SARPANIT, their "star-goddess mother of vegetation and fertility." And sure enough *"Eru"* is an Akkadian word for "pregnancy."

* * *

For nearly two millennium, MARDUK and SARPANIT are national patrons of all priest-magicians and priestesses of Babylonia. In fact, by literal title, "Babylon" became the *"seat of the gods,"* but by Mardukite standards, this was to be realized differently than either *monotheism* or *polytheism*.

The system of myth and magic born in Babylon was first and foremost dedicated to MARDUK's *"Divine World Order,"* often illustrated through the first mystical *"kabbalah"* system: *10 gates, 2 doors* and *7 levels*—just like the design for the Mardukite *ziggurat* "E.TEMEN.AN.KI" – *The Temple of Heaven and Earth*.

An excellent incantation-tablet example invokes MARDUK and SARPANIT after an experience of "evil from an eclipse," as first excavated by the French and transliterated in Vincent Scheil's *"Une Saison de Fouilles a Sippar,"* later translated by Thomson, who explains to us in *"Semitic Magic"* that the prayer was given to *King Assurbanipal* by his brother, *Samas-sumukin*. Both scholarly sources were used to reconstruct the full prayer in tact with both *English* and *French* translations of the original *Cuneifom* transliteration—

... O great lady, kindly mother,
   FR. ôo grande déesse, mère miséricordieuse
      C. *beltu sa-qu-ti ummu rim-ni-ti*

Amid the many stars of heaven,
   FR. parmi les nomlbreuses étoiles clu ciel
      C. *ina ma'-du-ti kakkabe sa-ma-mi*

Thou art mistress ...
   FR. vous êtes reine ...
      C. *beltu ka-a-si* ...

I, *Samas-sum-ukin*, the king, servant of his god
   FR. moi Samas sum ukîn roi, serviteur de son dieu
      C. *ana-ku Samas sum ukin sarru, GAL ili-su*

Vicegerent of his god Marduk and his goddess Sarpanit
   FR. vicaire de son dieu Marduk et de sa déesse Zarpanitum,
      C. *sakin ili-su (ilu)-Marduk (ilu)-Istarti-su (ilu)-Zar-pa-ni-tum*

Of the evils of the eclipse of the moon, Fixed for the fifteenth day of Shebat
>   FR. des maux de l'éclipse de lune fixée au 15 du mois d'AB
>   C. *ana lumun AN-MI (ilu)-Sin sa ina arhi AS um 15 (kam) sak-nu*

Of the evils of the signs and omens, evil, baneful,
>   FR. des maux de signes et visions funestes, malfaisantes
>   C. *ana lumun idati SI-BIT-mes limnuti la tabuti*

Which have occurred in palace and my land
>   FR. qui arriveraient dans mon palais et mon pays,
>   C. *sa ina e-kal-ya (MU) u mati-ya ibba-su*

I am afraid, and I fear, and I tremble
>   FR. j'ai peur, je tremble, je frémis
>   C. *pal-ha-ku-ma ad-ra-ku u su-ta-du-ra-ku*

Let not these evils draw near to me or my house
>   FR. ces maux, de moi et de ma maison
>   C. *lumnu suatu ya-a-si u biti-ya*

[. . .] "Let them not approach [come near]"
>   FR. qu'ils n'approchent pas
>   C. *a-a TE*

Accept the *upuntu*-plant from me and receive my prayer.
>   FR. agrée l'tpuntu, agrée ma prière
>   C. *upuntu muh-ri-in-ni-ma li-ki-e un-ni-ni*

What becomes apparent when researching Mardukite-specific materials: MARDUK is the original "rebel-god," rising to supremacy and places himself in the highest positions—"Primordial Dragonslayer" and "Creator of the Universe"—*Jupiter*—the great force that maintains the orderly zones of the "solar system." His domain evolves to include all sciences and magics—the true understanding of the hidden patterns and secret doctrines of the cosmos. It is here that all magical traditions were born—later fragmented into systems practiced throughout human history, and all based in symbols and signs, names and numbers, prayers and incantations. These are the esoteric or "*Hermetic*" arts first known to ENKI, then MARDUK, and finally NABU. The challenge of the "*Marduk Gate*" is then to actually apply the esoteric formulas of "Cosmic Law" to direct and channel the powers of the Universe toward causal manifestations in creation and personal ascension—otherwise true "*magic*."

The occult editor Simon relays in his handbook—

> "Where *Nergal* represents Will—pure Will, unassuaged by purpose—and *Inanna*, desire; *Marduk* is the Law. This Law is no so much the Law of courts and decrees, but the Law of science, the lineaments of the created universe. Through the first five Gates we have become initiated into the use and sense of various Forces; in the *Sixth Gate* we become masters at manipulating all of them, at mixing them to produce various effects."

Mardukite "initiates" actually invoke this current in numerous ways. However, in maintaining consistency with our current volume, it is the incantation-prayer tablets we are most interested, and there are many. Several "prayers" to MARDUK may be found in *"Necronomicon: The Anunnaki Bible."* The traditional "Gate Invocation" generally follows the formula demonstrated in the key examples from the *Kuyunjik* collection that the current editor has chosen to adapt for this series. The *"Isagila"* mentioned in its text is a reference to the primary ziggurat-temple of MARDUK in Babylon, also transliterated: E.SAG.ILU or *Esaggadhu*.

> Siptu gaasru supuuu iziz Assur
> Almighty, powerful and strong one of *Assur*.
>
> *Rubu tiizkaru bukur NU.DIM.MUD*
> Exalted, noble-blood, firstborn of *Enki*.
>
> *Marduk salbabu muris I.TUR.RA*
> Almighty *Marduk*, who causes the *Itura* to rejoice.
>
> *Bil I.SAG.ILA tukultiti Babiliki raim I.ZID.DA*
> Lord of the *Isagila*, Aid to Babylon, Lover of the *Izida*.
>
> *Musalim napistiti asarid I.MAH.TIL.LA mudussuubalatu*
> Preserver of Life, Prince of *Imahtilla*, Renewer of Life.
>
> *Zulul maati gamil nisi rapsaati*
> Shadow over the Land, Protector of foreign lands.
>
> *Usumugal kalis parakkani*
> Forever is [*Marduk*] the Sovereign of Shrines.

Sumuka kalis ina pi nisi taaab
  Forever is [*Marduk*] the name in the mouth of the people.

Marduk bilu rabuu ina kibitka kabitti luublut
  Almighty *Lord Marduk* at your command I remain alive.

Ina kibitika sirti luublut luuslimma
  At your command let me live, let me be perfect, let me behold your Divinity.

Luustammar iluutka
  What I will to be, let me obtain my wishes.

Ima usaammaru luuksuud
  [*Marduk*], cause righteousness to come from my mouth.

Supsika damiktimtim inalibbiya
  [*Marduk*], cause mercy to dwell in my heart.

Tiru u naanzazu likbuu damiktimtim
  Return to Earth, establish yourselves and command mercy.

Iliya liizziz ina imniya
  May my god stand at my right hand.

Istariya liizziz ina sumiliya
  May my goddess stand at my left hand.

Iliya sallimu ina idiya luukaaian
  May my god who is favorable to the stars, stand firmly at my side.

Surgamma kabaa simaa u magara
  To speak the Word of Command, to hear my prayer and show favor.

Amat akabbuu ima akabbuu luu maagrat
  When I speak, let the words by powerful.

Marduk bilu rabuu napistimtim kibi
  Almighty *Lord Marduk*, come and command life.

Balat napistiya kibi
  As you command my Life

Maharka namris adalluka luusbi
  Before you I bow, let me be satisfied

Bil urrula Ia litiska
  Bel's Fires go with you, *Ia* [*Enki*] smile upon you

Ilani sa kissati likrubuka
  May the Earth Gods be favorable to thee and me

Ilani rabuti libbaka litibu
  May the Good Gods delight in your mercy.

This incantation tablet continues on its reverse with part of a prayer addressing SARPANIT as the:

Queen of *Isagila*, the palace of the gods, the . . . mountain
  sar-rat I.SAG.ILA ikal ilani sa-du-u- . . .

Lady of Babylon, the Shadow of lands!
  Bi-lit Babili-ki su-lul ma-ta-a-ti

Lady of the gods, who loves to give life,
  ilu-Bilit ili sa bul-lu-ta i-ram-mu

Who gives succor in sorrow and distress,
  it-ti-rat ina puski u dannati

The . . . one, who holds the hand of . . .
  . . . *-ma-li-tu sa-bi-ta kata-du na-as-ki*

Who supports the weak, who pours out seed,
  i-pi-rat in-si sa-pi-kat ziru

Who protects life, who gives offspring and seed,
  na-si-rat napisti(ti) nadnat(at) aplu u ziru

Who bestows life, who takes away sighing, who accepts prayer,
  ka-i-sat balatu li-kat un-ni-ni ma-hi-rat tas-lit

Who has made the people, the whole of creation!
  ba-na-at nisi gi-mir nab-ni-ta

— 7 —
: NINIB-NINURTA :
SATURN – WHO COMPLETES THE FOUNDATION

Drawing from more readily available 19th Century "Assyriology" research, Simon's *"Necronomicon"* from the 1970's describes the Guardian of the *"Seventh Gate"* as the "youngest son" of ENLIL. The name given is ADAR, coupled with a footnote that the force is sometimes called NINIB. The remaining description is actually of a "storm-god" (not *Saturn*) and immediately the name ADAD comes to mind—the "storm god" and "youngest son" of ENLIL according to Sumerian tradition. So... Perhaps the author has made a mistake—some kind of typo. And what a critical point to have such obscurity: when we are on the brink of the final gate before reaching communion with the IGIGI—the *"Outer Ones."* Even many of the original Mardukite researchers misappropriated this energy current to ADAD-ISHKUR or *Ramman*—the "wind-storm deity." This has been officially corrected in our archives.

As it turns out, ambiguity of ancient "Mardukite" records was not an oversight. The personage of NINIB-ADAR is intentionally minimized for the Babylonian system. Confusing the "youngest son" of ENLIL with his "oldest son"—born to half-sister NINHURSAG or NINMAH—kept political attention away from any claims to "Enlilite" supremacy in Babylon. In Babylon, MARDUK was supreme—any access to a further *"Seventh Gate"* would require his direct assistance. In short—ADAR is not a typo of ADAD, but is in fact, the *Assyrian* (and in some cases, *Akkadian*) name derived from *Nindar* or NINURTA—the Anunnaki heir of ENLIL and representation of *Saturn* in Sumerian tradition.

Superseding all previous esoteric regards, it is NINURTA who is selected by the Sumerian Anunnaki to give watch of the *"Saturn Gate."* Clearly this provided inspiration for MARDUK to assume the *"Fifty Names"*—all of the "Keys to the Kingdom"—under his name. Modern occult "self-initiates" of the earlier "Simon" work are aware that passing the *"Marduk Gate"* allows a magician-priest of "Mardukite" tradition access to the *"Fifty Names"*— meaning direct access to the *"Arts of Civilization"* and *"Secret Formulas of the Cosmos."* Most seekers of the "New Age" are concerned with little else. For most who are diligent enough to seriously work through the gate-system, their work self-honestly ends here.

Those who may have thought they had completed some type of "Ascension" journey through *"Gates of the Necronomicon,"* using virtually all previously available lore, now discover they did not.

Naturally, very few modern practitioners have achieved "True Enlightenment" via a Mesopotamian revival of any kind when using materials other than what is available from the *Mardukite Research Organization*. Without the "Mardukite" foundation, other revivals become fanciful and imaginative reenactments that elevate consciousness to the same extent as any cultural-motif "New Age" creative visualization exercise. MARDUK makes *himself* the "final gate" of the material systems without actually being so. And those who *do* pass on from the *"Marduk Gate"* do not always even reach NINURTA—*Saturn*—withholding, in part, a complete spiritual progression all due to a political "cover-up" in Babylon, concealing any knowledge of NINURTA as the Sumerian heir to *Enlilship* of the local system.

To understand the ambiguity, one must realize that NINURTA does not even originally appear in the Sumerian "Olympian" *Pantheon of Twelve* and it seems his position among the "younger pantheon" on the *"Ladder of Lights"* is jumbled for later "Mardukite" followers. We must assume this was to prevent Sumerian succession from in any way "stealing the spotlight" from the position of MARDUK. Regarding the original Sumerian status of NINURTA and his absence from the pantheon, Zecharia Sitchin explains—

> *"Ninurta* was assigned the number 50, like his father. In other words, his dynastic rank was conveyed in a cryptographic message: If *Enlil* goes, you, *Ninurta*, step into his shoes; but until then, you are not one of the twelve, for the rank of '50' is occupied."

Among various excavated Sumerian tablet-cycles of KUR, the hero (or heroine) is attributed to one of three different characters—ENKI, INANNA and NINURTA—each encountering the force differently. The epic concerning NINURTA is the most detailed, possibly the most accurate, and bares striking resemblances to later Babylonian revisions (of the *"Enuma Elis"*) detailing MARDUK as the serpent-slayer next in line for *"Enlilship."* Loss of these details unfortunately led a broken spiritual system wrapped in Anunnaki politics. This is resolved in consciousness with a self-honest unification of the pantheon with "new" modern Mardukite standards of viewing the "younger generation" of Anunnaki gods. Doing this repairs a broken religio-magical system (or "spiritual paradigm"), now accessible to modern practitioners, scholars and esotericists for the very first time, *ever*—in a clarity not even known in the ancient world.

* * *

NINURTA is a hunter, but as a son of ENLIL we should not be surprised to find him described also as a "plough-man" or "farmer god." Many from the Enlilite lineage are connected to agriculture and "farming," much as the lineage of ENKI carries affinity for animals and "shepherding." In later Semtic lore, NINURTA appears as *Nimrod* (although this character is sometimes confused with NABU), sharing the same role as in older appearances from Mesopotamian literature—assisting in the reformation of civilization after the *Flood*. Politics enter the arena only when matters turn towards Babylon—NINURTA is actually the original organizer of Enlilite tribes against the Mardukites in Babylon. In one famous cuneiform epic, he is given the epithet "ISHUM"—from the "*Erra Epos*" cuneiform tablet cycle ("*Erra and Ishum*") described in a prior chapter—meaning "scorcher." He acts as an adviser to NERGAL (ERRA) during the violent acts to "unseat" MARDUK from Babylon.

Both NINURTA and his consort—BAU (or *Gula*)—are actually attributed healing properties in the original Sumerian mystical tradition. As the defeater of both "*Asag*" (or KUR) and ANZU (in another epic), NINURTA is called upon to "*defeat*" demons and "evil spirits"—of sickness and disease. BAU, especially, is a patron to nurses and doctors. At first glance, these attributes seem out of character as representations of the *Saturn*-current—which reflects a confrontation of the darkest ("hidden") parts of *ourselves* in combination with the final constraints of "Cosmic Law" as it applies to the local material system. The "absolute healing" seems more appropriate when we consider that the "*Saturn Gate*" is the final threshold crossing or barrier to "Ascension"—*liberation* from the material program—and its primary gatekeeper according to the Sumerian tradition, is NINURTA, the Anunnaki-decreed rightful heir to ENLIL. The very essence of a "*seven-fold*" system comes into logic focus more clearly than ever before—the "*Foundation of Heaven and Earth*" is complete and the mysteries of the ziggurat "Temple of the Seven Spheres" are laid out before the Seeker.

The "*Seventh Gate*" leads to the "*Supernal Trinity*" of Anunnaki—the "*outer limits*" of our local system—a position in which NINURTA is waiting for heir-ship of in the Sumerian system. This means by some standard, era or version: ENLIL, NINURTA *and* MARDUK all maintain the designation (position) of "50." The heart of this beats a difficult fact to accept for the bloodline of MARDUK and all those calling ENKI, "Father" in the *Mardukite* paradigm. All this may seem trite to the uninitiated, but it is probably the deepest darkest kept secret in ancient Babylon—thus, even there deserving of the designation of *Saturn*.

Proper realization of the system is what esotericists seek as the *"Hidden Key to the Necronomicon."* It not only brings harmony to the system for a modern practitioner—divine-messengers and temple-servants of the gods—but, for the gods *themselves*.

Mysteries of the *"Seventh Gate"* represent the highest initiation accessible to priests and priestesses *on earth*. More or less "divisions" of the whole does not change the whole. Others have simply broken down perceived fragments of reality into other *quantities*—the Babylonian "Gate-system" consists of *seven*. The "Secrets of the Gates" are hidden throughout Babylon in mythic sagas and esoteric traditions of *Elder Gods* and the *younger pantheon* in Mesopotamia.

On many levels of manifestation, the "Gates" *are* functional. The *"Hidden Key"*—the paradigm represented by the whole—was essentially the *first* "government-secret" kept by priests and scribes occupying the highest positions—the final "combination sequence" to make the "Star Gate of Babylon" actually *work*. Even as the "Seat" of MARDUK, by Sumerian standards, the existence of Babylon and MARDUK's "Star-Gate" was deemed "illegal" in Enlilite territory. Babylon was eventually destroyed—hence our misunderstood genetic memory of the *"Tower of Babylon"* incident. NINURTA held residence in several ancient Mesopotamian cities, but most scholars agree his primary ziggurat-temple was the *E.Shumedu* in Nippur.

NINURTA—as heir to ENLIL—was a "solar deity" representing *Saturn*, but also *Sirius* in the old Sumerian astrology, as did MARDUK later. *Sirius* is often referred to in mystical literature as the "sun behind the sun," and is considered the true and secret form of ancient "solar-worship." MARDUK sought to represent the same "sun behind the sun" in Egypt. As one cannot see a candle flame when placed in front of the sun—the elusive celestial force of *Sirius* is shared as "Saturn of Stars," and part of a gateway or bridge beyond our system.

The "Invocation of the Saturn Gate" dedicated to NINURTA previously used by modern Mardukite Chamberlains from *"Necronomicon: The Anunnaki Bible"* is effective, but another incantation example for esoteric experimentation or general research is included here as adapted from the second tablet of the "Prayers of the Lifting of the Hand" series—

>O mighty son, firstborn of ENLIL.
>*siptu ap-lu gas-ru bu-kur ilu-Bil*

Powerful, perfect offspring of ISARA,
sur-bu-u git-ma-lu i-lit-ti I.SAR.RA

Who art clothed with terror, who art full of fury!
sa pu-luh-tu lit-bu-su ma-lu-u har-ba-su

O NINURTA, whose onslaught is unopposed!
ilu-NIN.UR.TA [sa la im]-mah-ha-ru ka-bal-su

Mighty is thy place among the great gods!
su-bu-u man-[za-za] ina ilani rabuti

In E.KUR, the house of decisions, exalted are thee,
ina I.KUR bit ta-[si]-la-a-ti sa-ka-a ri-sa-a-ka

And ENLIL, thy father has granted thee
id-din-ka-ma ilu-Bil abu-ka

The law of all the gods thy hand should hold!
ti-rit kul-lat ilani ka-tuk-ka tam-hat

Thou judges the judgment of mankind!
ta-dan di-in ti-ni-si-i-ti

Thou leads him that is without a leader, the man that is in need.
tus-ti-sir la su-su-ru i-ka-a i-ku-ti

Thou holds the hand of the weak, you raise him that is not strong!
ta-sab-bat kat [in-si] la li-'-a tu-sa-as-ka

The body of the man that to the Lower World has been brought down, you can restore!
sa a-na a-ra-al-[li]-i su-ru-du pa-gar-su tutira-ra-

From him who sin possesses, the sin you can remove!
sa ar-nu i-su-u ta-pat-tar ar-nu

Thou art quick to favor the man with whom the god is angry.
sa ilu-su itti-su zi-nu-u tu-sal-lam ar-his

O NINIB, prince of the gods, a hero you are!
ilu-NIN.IB a-sa-rid ilani ku-ra-du at-ta

I, so and so, son of, so and so, whose god is so and so, whose goddess is so and so,
ana-ku pulanu apil pulani sa ilu-su pulanu ilu-istari-su pulanitum(um)

Have bound for thee a cord, . . . [a cord]. . . have I offered thee;
ar-kus-ka rik-sa ku.a.tir as-ruk-ka

I have offered thee *tarrinnu*, a pleasant odor;
as-ruk-ka tar-[rin]-nu u-ri-su tabu

I have poured out for thee mead, a drink from corn.
akki-ka du-us-su-bu si-kar as-na-an

With the may there stand the gods of ENLIL.
itti-ka li-iz-zi-zu ilani su-ut ilu-Bil

With thee may there stand the gods of E.KUR!
itti-ka li-iz-zi-zu ilani su-ut I.KUR

Truly pity me and hearken to my cries!
ki-nis nap-lis-an-ni-[ma si-mi] la-ba-ai

My sighing remove and accept my supplication!
un-ni-ni-ya [li-ki-ma mu-hur] tas-lit

Let my cry find acceptance before thee!
zik-ri [li-tib] ili-ka

Deal favorably with me who fear thee!
si-lim itti ya-a-tu-u pa-lih-ka

Thy face have I beheld, let me have prosperity!
pa-ni-ka a-ta-mar lu-si-ra ana-ku

Thou art full of pity. Truly pity me!
[mu]-up-pal-sa-ta ki-nis nap-lis-an-ni

Take away my sin, remove my iniquity!
an-ni pu-tur sir-ti pu-sur

Tear away my disgrace and my offenses you loosen!
[i]-ti-ik kil-la-ti-ma hi-ti-ti ru-um-[mi]

May my god and goddess command me and may they ordain
  good fortune!
  [ili]-ya u ilu-istari-ya li-sa-ki-ru-in-ni-ma lik-bu-u damiktim(tim)

May I praise thy heart, I bow in humility before thee.
  [lib]-bi-ka lu-sa-pi da-li-li-ka lud-lul

—APPENDIX—
THE SUMERIAN LEGACY

— A —
: MESOPOTAMIAN MATHEMATICS :
SECRETS OF MEASURING SPACE AND TIME

Ancient Sumerians observed and understood connections between cycles, time and mathematics. In addition to the "invention" and pragmatic use of the "wheel" (or circle), they also developed "religious" calculations of the circle at 360-degrees. Their use of "Base-60" or "*sexagesimal*" math for systematic measurement of time-space remains with humanity to this present day.

Consider the length of a day at 24-hours (or two sets of twelve) of "60"-minutes containing "60"-seconds each; or the celestial zones of the astrological zodiac as a "wheel" or sphere of twelve "houses" of 30 degrees each; or else the twelve 30-day "festivals of the moon" composing an annual cycle or "wheel of the year"—or "*sat-ti.*" The annual year (*sat-ti*) was even originally only divided into three seasons: beginning ("*res sat-ti*"), middle ("*misil sat-ti*") and end ("*kit sat-ti*").

"Magicians" and esoteric philosophers—ancient and modern—find significance in sigil-scripts, colors, mystical alphabets and other "occult correspondences." All of these play their parts in magical ritual drama, spiritual incantations and other ceremonial applications. As a *universal* expression of "Cosmic Law," *numbers* are the most fundamental mystical "signs" in the realm of form, representing infinite wisdom and practical correspondences. Although our traditional or more familiar "classical" system of numerology is derived from a "Base-10" paradigm (for example, where "10x10=100" is a *whole*), the original Mesopotamian mathematics is "Base-6," or more appropriately, "Base-60." This only seems complicated because modern consciousness is most familiar with a "*Base-10 metric system*"—decades and centuries and "percents."

In Western civilization, "Base-60" mathematics is most closely identified with our sense of "time." Rather than dividing an hour into hundredths or percents, we are able to see 60-minutes as the "*whole pie.*" A quarter of that "pie," while still "25%"—per-*cent*, meaning "per-*100*"—it is *not* a quantified value of "25," but instead: "15," as in 15-minutes—"15x4=60." The modern standard space-measuring "foot" is divided by 12—and "12x5=60." This type of thinking more closely resembles Mesopotamian worldview.

Although school-teachers most frequently emphasize only the proverbial Sumerian "use of the wheel," it was the "mathematics" that forever established that the wheel (or more correctly, the "circle") consisted of 360-degrees—or "6x60=360." Here among the ancients, "geometry" was born—long before the classical Greek mathematicians—a means of literal "earth-measuring." Even more than this, the ancients demonstrated abilities to measure time-space on "earth," in the "heavens" and the relationships between.

BASIC MESOPOTAMIAN MATHEMATICAL FORMULAS

6 x 1	= 6	= earth, fire, power, spatial [*Marduk*]
6 x 10	= 60	= command, heaven-earth, fire [*Anu*]
6 x 10 x 10	= 600	= chaos, void, abyss, dragon [*Tiamat*]
6 x 60	= 360	= earth-time, cycles ["*local planet*"]
6 x 60 x 6	= 2160	= earth meets heaven ["*zodiacal age*"]
6 x 60 x 10	= 3600	= heaven-time, spiritual cycles ["*sar*"]

A full turn or cycle of the "Wheel of the Year"—"*sat-ti*"—in *Babylonia* was separated into "12 periods" (or *zones*) of 30-days (*degrees*) each. These periods equated to 12 annual "*moonth festivals*," more appropriately called "months." The quantity values of 12x30 and 6x60 are identical—*360*. Ancient astronomers were also aware that the observed year was actually slightly longer than 360-days, and that there are actually 13 lunar cycles in a year, so an additional "*13th month*" was included to make the calculations fit the observations. Everything is always in motion. We must even rectify the mathematics of our modern linear time-keeping with the inclusion of "leap-days." In most instances of the ancient calendar, a "*new moon*" meant the start of a "*new month*." The days counted of a month were synonymous with the "days of the moon"—for example: "*sixth day of the moon.*"

SUMERIAN/AKKADIAN ANNUAL YEAR

1. Nisannu – Nisan (*spring equinox*)
2. Airu – Iyyar
3. Simanu – Siwan
4. Du'uzu – Tammuz
5. Abu – Ab
6. Ululu – Elul
7. Tishritu – Tisri (*autumn equinox*)

8. Arahsamna – Marchesvan
9. Kislimu – Kislev
10. Tebitu – Tebet
11. Shabatu – Sebat
12. Addau – Adar
13. "Second Adar" (*extra month*)

CELESTIAL SPHERE CONSTELLATIONS ("ZODIAC")

1. Ku-mal (*Aries*)
2. Gu-an-na (*Taurus*)
3. Mash-tab-ba (*Gemini*)
4. Dub (*Cancer*)
5. Ur-gula (*Leo*)
6. Ab-sin (*Virgo*)
7. Zi-bi-an-na (*Libra*)
8. Gir-tab (*Scorpio*)
9. Pa-bil (*Sagittarius*)
10. Su-hur-mash (*Capricorn*)
11. Gu (*Aquarius*)
12. Sim-mah (*Pisces*)

The annual cycle was also divided as a light and dark half, marked distinctly by the two primary religious festivals of ancient Mesopotamia—the spring festival of *Akitu* and the harvest festival of *Zagmuk*. Both are symbolically represented as points of "*divine marriage*" between "heaven" and "earth"—later signifying simply the relationship between a ruling King and his lands. Originally, the more popular *fertility rites* of the spring were agricultural, with an emphasis on *land renewal*. With later development and spread of these tradition, *Akitu* became known as *Ostara*—the pagan *Easter*—in dedication to ISHTAR (*Inanna*).

Mesopotamian mathematics is "*sexagesimal.*" The number "sixty"—attributed to ANU—is sacred within its own system, with exactly *twelve* factors—*three* of which are prime. These "factors" also appear in the tradition as *sacred* numbers—1, 2, 3, 4, 5, 6, 10, 12, 15, 20, 30 and itself, 60. It is perhaps no small coincidence that "60" is the smallest whole number value perfectly divisible by all of the numbers 1 through 6. This was very useful in the highly innovative form of "*multiplication by reciprocal*" developed by the Sumerians and Babylonians.

Logic calculations requiring a value to be "divided" by another number, were instead written as a "multiplication" of the reciprocal (or inverse) of the other number—"60 *divided by* 10" becomes "60 *multiplied by* one-tenth."

$$[60 / 10 = 6] \text{ is the same as } [60 \times 0.1 = 6]$$

Calculations of space and distance also followed *sexagesimal* patterns. Where we are familiar today with the use of centimeters and inches, feet and yards, the basic unit of length measurement in ancient Mesopotamia was essentially the division of a meter (*"kush"*) into 360-parts called a *she*, each equivalent to approximately one-tenth of an inch. If we simply transfer a decimal place, we can still use the "standard" system to visualize—where one foot or 12-inches approximately equals 120 *she*, so 1 *kush* or 360 *she* is roughly equivalent to 36-inches. [It is interesting that society has retained a system of spatial-measure where a standard unit is divided into 12-parts.]

6 *she*	=	1 *su-shi*
30 *su-shi* or 360 *she*	=	1 *kush*

The original Anunnaki hierarchy of pantheon designations runs in increments of five—from 5 to 60—allowing space for the "Olympian Twelve" to be plotted thereupon. The Sumerian Anunnaki *"Pantheon of Twelve"* of course consists of: *Anu* (60), *Antu* (55), *Enlil* (50), *Ninlil* (45), *Enki* (40), *Ninki-Damkina* (35), *Nanna* (30), *Ningal* (25), *Shammash* (20), *Inanna-Ishtar* (15), *Ishkur-Adad* (10) and *Ninhursag-Ninmah* (5). Spiritual politics in post-Sumerian Mesopotamia resulted when altering the names (or representative figures) with the "Mardukite" pantheon, but the actual "roles" themselves went unchanged—mathematically fixed. Designations for the *"Supernal Trinity"*—60, 50 and 40—become "master numbers" of Babylonian numerology. The fractional designations for the *"planetary gates"* are inherited by the "younger pantheon" in Babylon—

PRECESSION OF BABYLONIAN GATES

1 = 7	Nanna – 30	30 x 2 = 60	30 = 1 / 2 x 60 (Moon)
2 = 6	Nabu – 12	12 x 5 = 60	12 = 1 / 5 x 60 (Mercury)
3 = 5	Ishtar – 15	15 x 4 = 60	15 = 1 / 4 x 60 (Venus)
4 = 4	Samas – 20	20 x 3 = 60	20 = 1 / 3 x 60 (Sun)
5 = 3	Nergal – 8		(Mars)
6 = 2	Marduk – 10	10 x 6 = 60	10 = 1 / 6 x 60 (Jupiter)
7 = 1	Ninurta – 4	4 x 15 = 60	4 = 1 / 15 x 60 (Saturn)

— B —
: MARDUKITE SIGIL-SEALS OF THE ANUNNAKI :
FROM "NECRONOMICON: ANUNNAKI BIBLE" (TABLET-X)

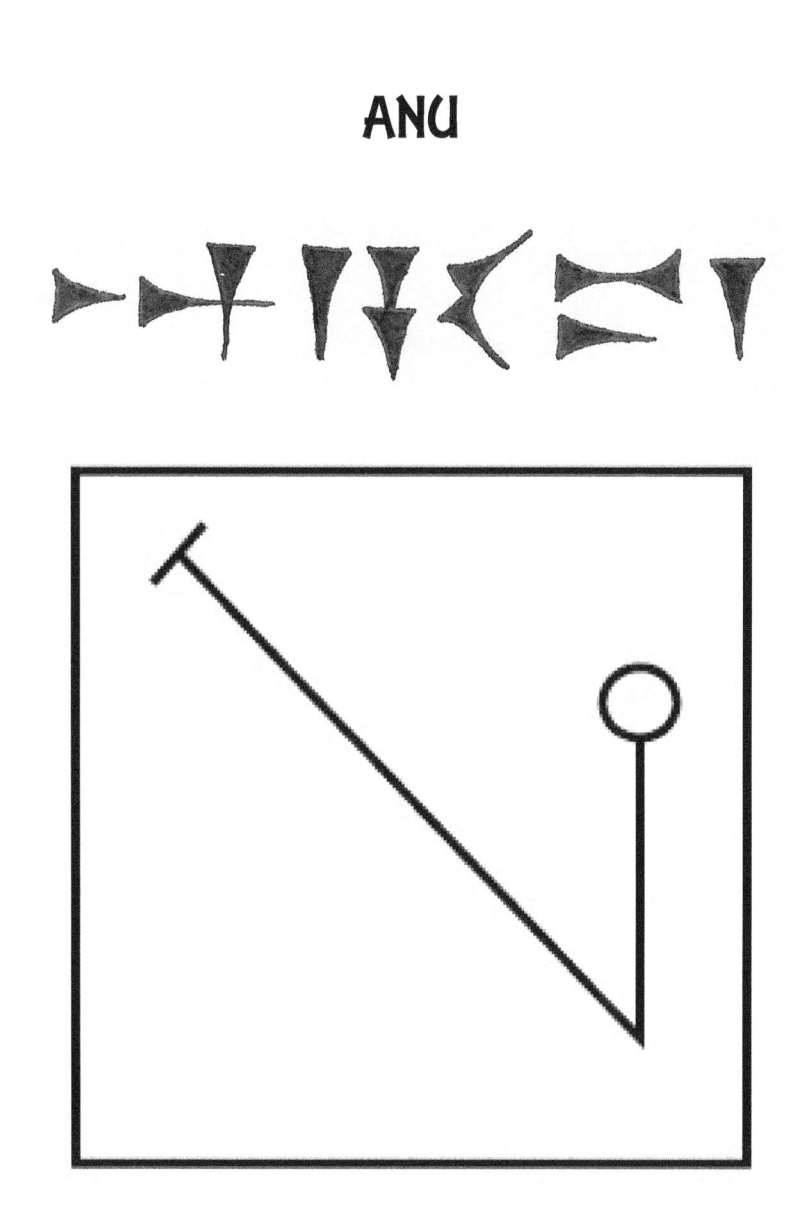

ANU

ENLIL

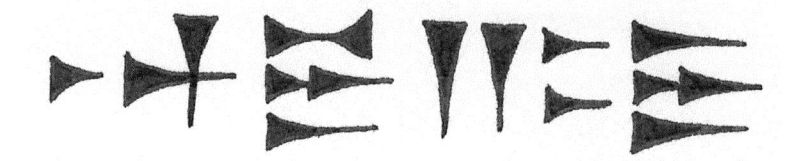

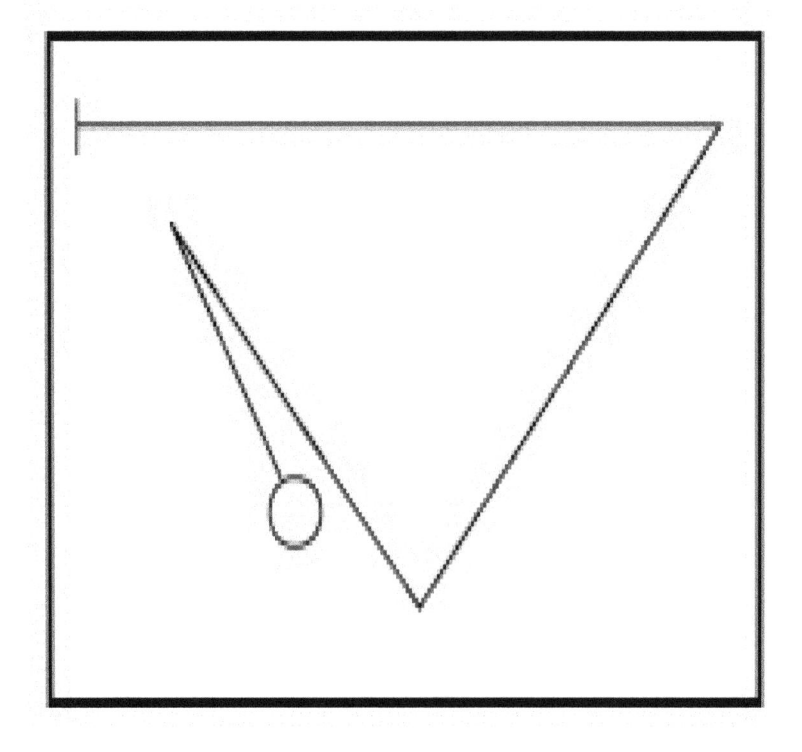

ENKI

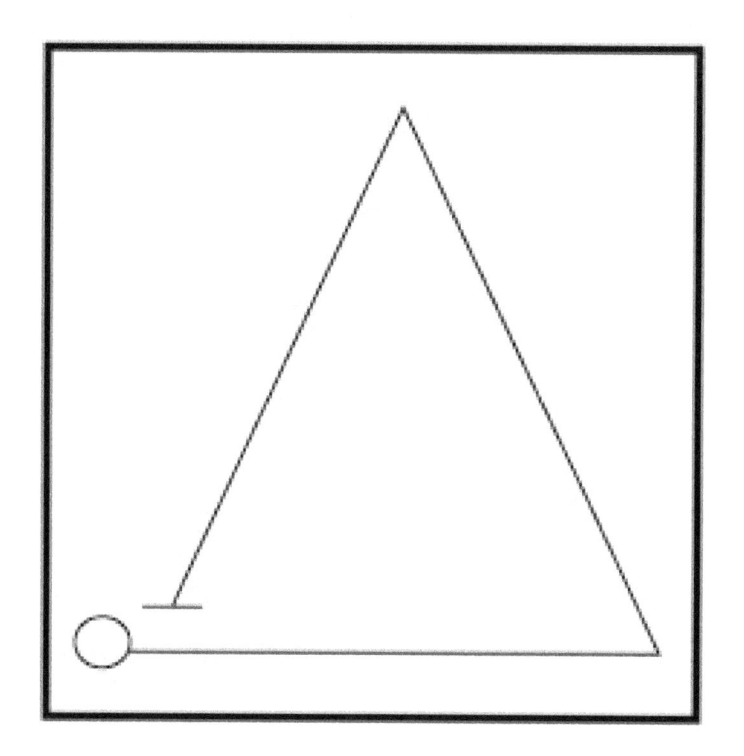

NANNA

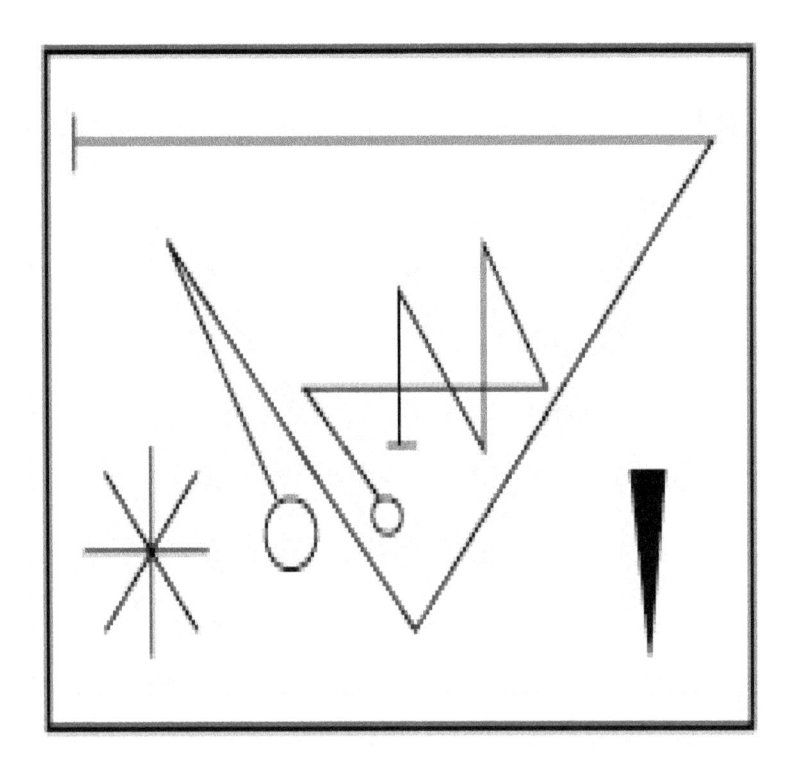

NABU

ISHTAR

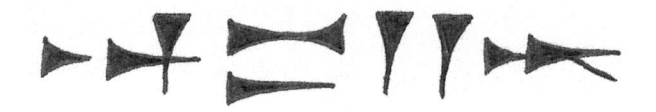

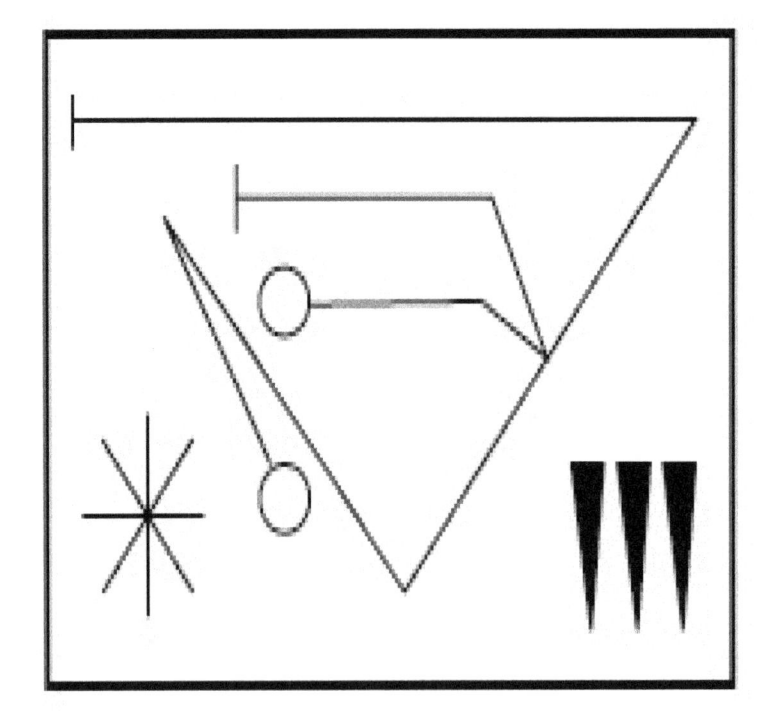

SAMAS

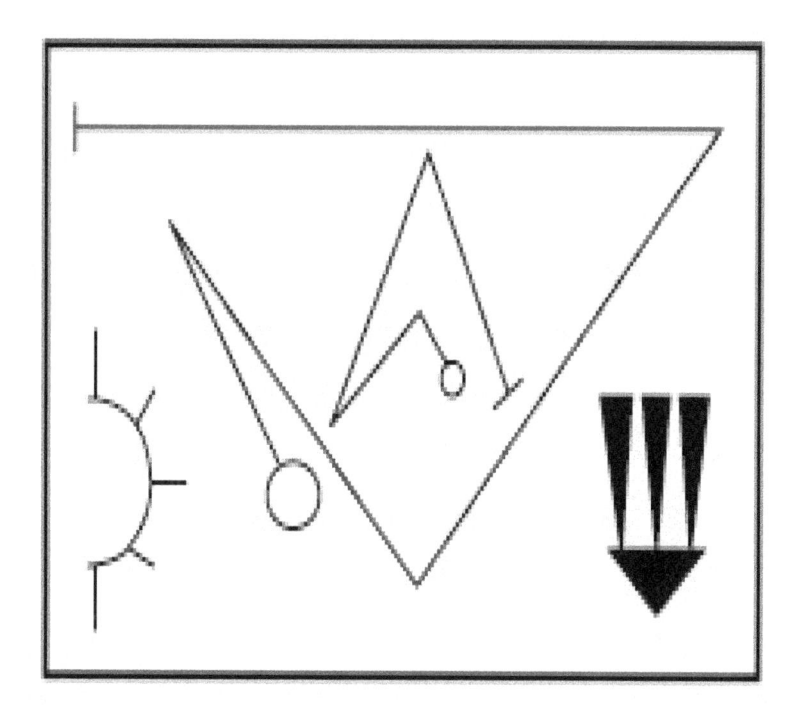

NERGAL

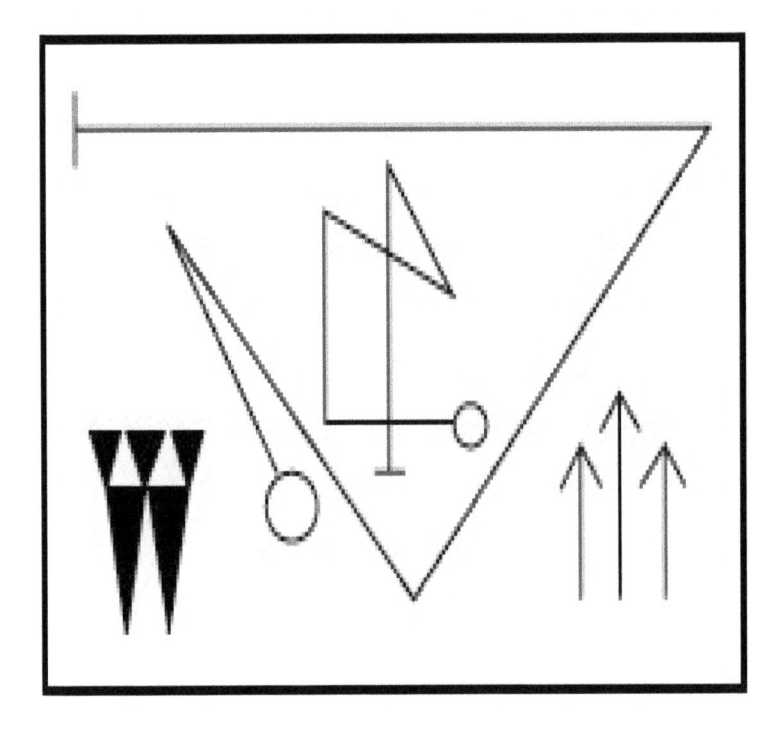

MARDUK

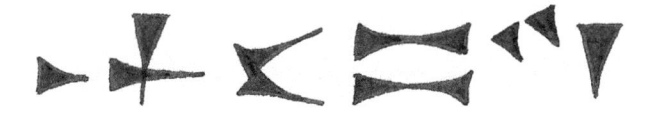

NINURTA (NINIB)

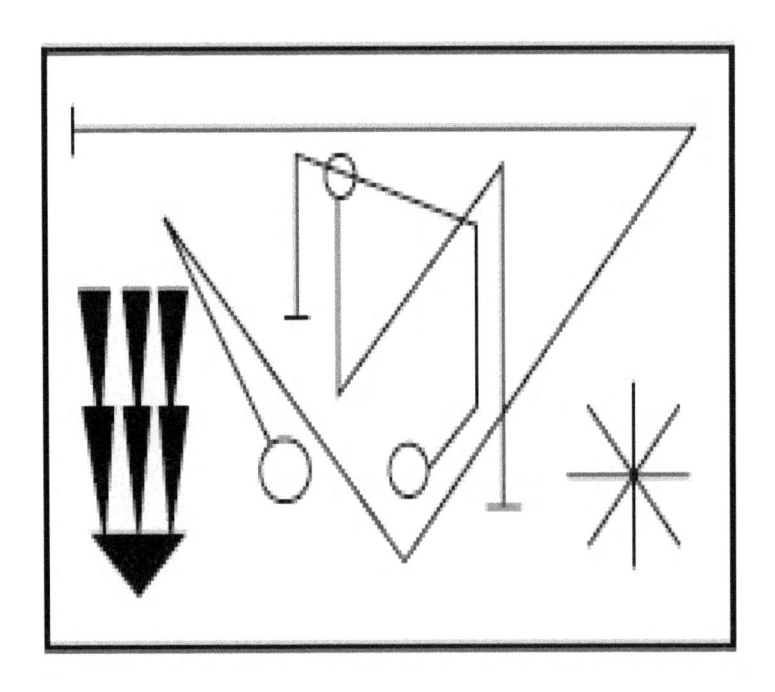

SARPANIT

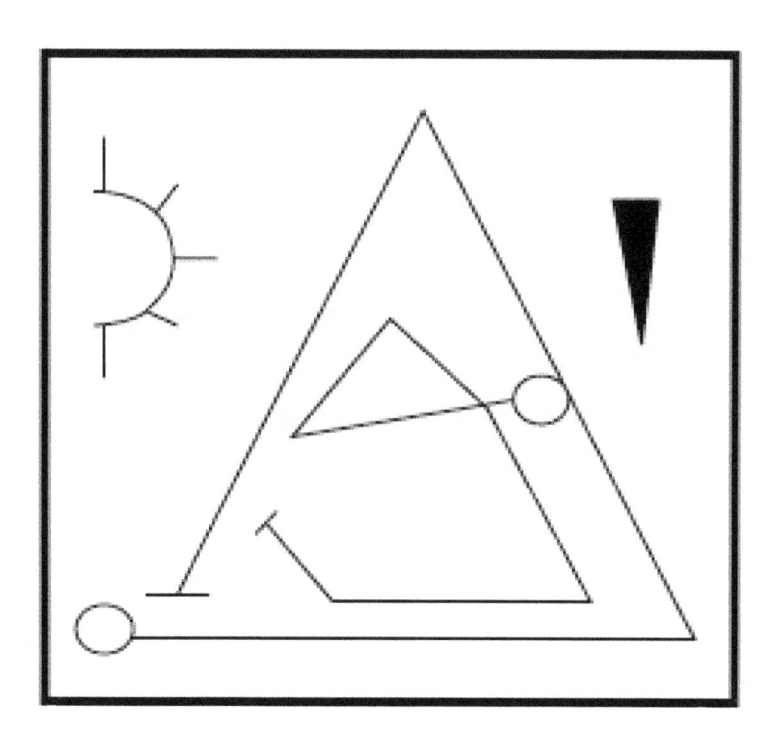

— ☾ —
: BOOK OF MARDUK BY NABU :
FROM "NECRONOMICON: ANUNNAKI BIBLE" (TABLET-W)

We have sealed seven representative stations in BABYLON. While it is true that each of the cities did emphasize their local patrons, a god and a goddess, We have sought a unity for all the gods, under the watchful eye of my father, MARDUK, son of ENKI.

Our father, ENKI, took MARDUK as an apprentice to the magical and religious arts while in E.RIDU and I later took hold of such mysteries and dispersed the knowledge to my scribes and priests in BABYLON and Egypt, where my family was recognized by other names.

The "Seven" are each embodiments of one of the seven gates forged in BABYLON, homes to the gods of the "younger pantheon." It is true, the same seven-fold division may be found to fragment the *world of form*—corresponding to color, sound, or the planets observed by the ancient ancestors from Earth, seen as *"Guardians."* The seven planetary systems, which have been connected to the "Seven" of the Gates, also correlate to an easily observable weekly cycle of time. The planet-ruling days will offer the supplicant [priest] an intention ceremonial or meditative opportunity to appeal to each of the "sets" of ANUNNAKI "divine couples" honored in the "younger pantheon" of Babylon.

> Sunday – Sun – SHAMMASH [UTU] (& AYA)
> Monday – Moon – NANNA [SIN] (& NINGAL)
> Tuesday – Mars – NERGAl (& ERESHKIGAL)
> Wednesday – Mercury – NABU (& TESHMET)
> Thursday – Jupiter – MARDUK (& SARPANIT)
> Friday – Venus – ISHTAR [INANNA] (& DUMUZI)
> Saturday – Saturn – NINIB [NINURTA] (& BA'U)

Within the combined domains of the "Seven" are all of the material and spiritual aspects a priest, priestess or magician seeks in life (e.g. ISHTAR for *love* or SAMAS for *truth*) and one merely must appeal with self-honesty and true words to attain them. This is as the original arts were set down in days of old, left for men to remember us—and we will remember you.

The names and Gates are not merely there for the bedazzlement of the "occult initiate" as you have been taught (there to ascend to and forget about): they are very real "magical skills" and "spiritual lessons" based on the division and fragmentation of the material universe—a mastery only attainable by a true and faithful relationship with the ANUNNAKI gods of your ancestors.

Man's use of the spiritual power of the gods became subverted, altered and bastardized into the mystical systems now given for your disposal, written by men with no better understanding of the traditions they seek to invoke then those who read them. (And some of these traditions have even falsely said to be derived from my hand.) The true priest, priestess or magician compels the gods by friendship and trust, not fear and hatred. By MARDUK, I learned the power of incantation. I was taught to appease the gods in his name, to speak the words of the higher. MARDUK invoked the name of ENKI, our father, who, invoked the name of ANU. And so was born the magical "hierarchies" that magicians have confused. I taught the magician-scribes of my order to invoke my name and seal during their petitions to the gods, which I have given here, as I learned it from MARDUK.

> *ANU above me, King in Heaven.*
> *ENLIL, Commander of the Airs.*
> *ENKI, Lord of the Deep Earth.*
> *I am NABU – hear my words.*
> *I am the priest of MARDUK and SARPANIT.*
> *Son of our father, ENKI and DAMKINA.*
> *I am the priest in E.RIDU.*
> *I am the magician in BABYLON.*
> *My spell is the spell of ENKI.*
> *My incantation is the incantation of MARDUK.*
> *The Tablets of Destiny, I hold in my hands.*
> *The Ankh of ANU and ANTU, I hold in my hands.*
> *The wisdom of ENLIL and NINLIL, I call to me.*
> *The Magic Circle of ENKI and DAMKINA, I conjure about me.*
> *SHAMMASH and AYA are before me.*
> *NANNA-SIN and NINGAL are behind me.*
> *NERGAL and ERESHKIGAL are at my right side.*
> *NINIB-NINURTA and BA'U are at my left side.*
> *The blessed light of ISHTAR and DUMUZI shines favorably upon my sacred work.*
> *It is not I, but MARDUK, who performs the incantations.*

As should become increasingly apparent to the the contemporary folk of the current age, the ANUNNAKI are powerful and influential, though often directly unseen, forces behind the reality of the life you exist in—as your ancestors were well aware of. If you work with us in conjunct-ion with the natural flow of the universal energies, then you will come face to face with your true destiny—and invited home, again.

Discern your true-knowledge, learn the challenge of self-mastery, and then dear *seeker*, resolve to walk with the gods among the stars, circumnavigating the illusions of this world which have been raised before you as a test of your existence. When you have proven yourself before us, we shall celebrate your arrival...

MONDAY – THE MOON – NANNA & NINGAL

ilu-NANNA. ilu-SIN. ilu-istari-NINGAL.
NANNA. SIN. NINGAL.
ilu-NANNAR. ilu-NAMRASIT.
NANNAR. MOON.
su-bu-u man-za-za ina ilani rabuti maru aplu ilu-ENLIL u ilu-NINLIL
Mighty One among the gods, son of ENLIL and NINLIL,
nam-rat urru-ka ina sami-i ina sat musi
Brightest in the heavens at night,
du natalu, nasaru anabu harranu-dim
Keeping watch, protecting weary travelers
u nisu ina bitu sat musi suttu
And the people in their homes as they sleep.
itti namrasit ina sami-i
Your brightness extends through the heavens,
kima diparu, kima ilu-SAMAS
Like a torch – Like a fire-god [Samas].
samsatu ilu-NANNA namaru suttu agu
Radiance of NANNA, who reflects the dreams of men,
abu ilu-SAMAS
Father of the SUN
rimi-nin-ni-ma anaku ____, apil ____, sa ilu-sa ____ u ilu-istari-su ____ .
Be favorable to me, I, __ son of __, whose god is __ and whose goddess is __ .
ilu-NANNA u ilu-NINGAL rimi-nin-ni-ma
May NANNA and NINGAL deal graciously with me,

kaparu anaku sillatu lu-us-tam-mar ilu-ut-ka
Cleanse me of iniquity that I may be free to call upon thee.
petu babu temu
Open the Gates of your mysteries to me,
li-iz-ziz ina imni-ya u sumuli-ya anaku arad-ka elu
Stand on either side of me, a servant of the Highest.
an-un-na-ki ti-i-ru u na-an-za-zu
May the ANUNNAKI come forth an be established.

TUESDAY – MARS – NERGAL & ERESHKIGAL

ilu-NERGAL. ilu-IRRIGAL. ilu-istari-ERESHKIGAL. ilu-ERRA.
NERGAL. IRRIGAL. ERESHKIGAL. ERRA. MARS.
siru belu ersetu
Exalted Lord of the Underworld.
ilu-istari-ERESHKIGAL, beltu ersetu
ERESHKIGAL, Queen of the Underworld.
saqu-su manzazu it-ti ilani samu
Great is your place among the gods of heaven.
ilu-NERGAL u ilu-istari-ERESHKIGAL
NERGAL and ERESHKIGAL,
rimi-nin-ni-ma, ana-ku ___ , apil ___ , sa ilu-su ___ ilu-istar-su ___ .
Truly have mercy on me, __ , son of ___ , whose god is ___ , whose goddess is ___ .
banu-ya libbu alalu
May your hearts be tempered.
di-ni uzzu ina ramanu libbu
Temper also the anger within my heart,
ana-ku izuzzu mahru ze
That I may stand before you,
petu babu temu
Open the Gates of your understanding to me.
rimi-nin-ni-ma ina damu u du lemnutu seg ina ramanu zi
Grant me a favorable death and keep evil from me in life.
ana-ku arad-ka elu kamazu ze rimi-nin-ni-ma
I, a servant of the Highest, kneel before thee, take pity on me.
babu-mah du pataru
May the Great Doors stand open.
an-un-na-ki ti-i-ru u na-an-za-zu
May the ANUNNAKI return and be established.

WEDNESDAY – MERCURY – NABU & TESHMET

ilu-NABU. ilu-TUTU. ilu-istari-TESHMET ilu-istari-TASMIT. ilu-NEBOS.
NABU. TUTU. TESHMET – TASMIT(U). NEBOS. MERCURIOS.
tupsarru si-mat ilani
Scribe among the Gods,
sarru nam-zu si-mat ilani
Keeper of the Wisdom of the Gods,
asaridu bukur ilu-MARDUK u ilu-SARPANIT
Firstborn of MARDUK and SARPANIT.
ilu-NABU na-as duppu si-mat ilani
NABU, Bearer of the Tablet of Destinies of the gods,
ramanu ur-hi suttu lid-mi-ik
May my dreams [destiny] be filled with prosperity.
ilu-NABU u ilu-TASMITU ka-ba-a si-ma-a suk-na ya-si-sa
May my petitions fall on the ears of NABU & TASMIT.
rimi-nin-ni-ma, ana-ku ___ , apil ___ sa ilu-sa ___ u ilu-istari-su ___ .
Be favorable to me, I, __ son of __ , whose god is __ and whose goddess is __ .
ebbu ramanu nam-eme-sig u ummuqu si-mi-i su-pi-ya
Cleanse me of false knowledge, that I might be ft to call upon thee.
petu babu temu
Open the Gates of your understanding to me.
amat a-kab-bu-u kima a-kab-bu-u lu-u ma-ag-rat
Bless my mouth with true words to speak the prayers
sumu-ka ka-lis ina pi nisi ta-a-ab
May the prayers rise from the lips of the people.
anaku arad-ka elu
I am a servant of the Highest,
an-un-na-ki ti-i-ru u na-an-za-zu
May the ANUNNAKI come forth and be established.

THURSDAY – JUPITER – MARDUK & SARPANIT

ilu-MAR.DUG. ilu-MAR.DUK. ilu-istari-ZARPANIT. Ilu-silik-MULU.KHI DIL.GAN.
MARDUK. MERODACH. SARPANIT. MULU-KHI. JUPITER.
lugal arali, belu asipu, ilu-su BAB.ILI
Lord of the Lands, Master of Magicians, God of Babylon.

ilu-SARPANIT(UM), belitu istari-su BAB.ILI
SARPANIT, Lady of Babylon.
gasru u sapsu ina an-ki zi atwu
Mighty and powerful on earth and heaven are your words.
belu u belitu su BAB.ILI
Lord and Lady of Babylon,
maharu ramanu arua abnu-gesnu, abnu-uqnu u hurasu
Accept my offerings of alabaster, lapis lazuli and gold.
dinu-ma ramanu lid-mi-ik
Judge my life favorably,
anaku ___ apil ___ sa ilu-su ___ u ilu-istar-su ___ .
I ___ , son of ___ , whose god is ___ , and whose goddess is ___ .
lu-us-tam-mar ilu-ut-ka u atwu ramanu maharu karabu
Make me fit to behold your divinity and teach me to receive thy blessings.
petu babu temu – petu babu idu
Open the Gates of your understanding. Open the gates of your power.
ina ki-bi-ti-ka sir-ti lu-ub-lut lu-us-lim-ma
Let me live. Let me be perfect.
napsiti narbu ramanu ki-bi su su-sud ilani samu
Command greatness in my life as your expansion permeates the gods of heaven.
anaku arad-ka elu
I am a servant of the Highest.
an-un-na-ki ti-i-ru u na-an-za-zu
May the ANUNNAKI come forth and be established.

FRIDAY – VENUS – ISHTAR & DUMUZI

ilu-INANNA. ilu-istari-ISHTAR. ilu-DUMUZI. ilu-ISTAR.
INANNA. ISHTAR. DUMUZI. ISTARI VENUS.
belitu, martu-su ilu-NANNA-SIN sa karabu ina samu
Queen, Daughter of the Moon, who is blessed by the heavens,
ramu-su ilu-ANU, rabianu samu
Beloved of ANU, Command in Heaven,
namru-sat musi
Brightness of the Evening,
lu-dub-gar-ra sat musi
Huntress of the Night,
li-iz-ziz ilu-istari-ya ina sumili-ya sutlumu karabu nissanu sabu u ilani
Do come to stand favorably at my side, grant me the fruits of men and gods.

ilu-istari-ISHTAR u ilu-DUMUZI
ISHTAR and DUMUZI,
rimi-nin-ni-ma, ana-ku ___ apil ___ sa ilu-sa ___ u ilu-istar-su ___
Be favorable to me, I, ___ son of ___, whose god is ___ and whose goddess is ___,
mesu-ya nigussu, anaku aga simtu maharu zi qistu
Cleanse me of impurity make me a vessel fit to receive your rewards.
petu babu temu
Open the Gates of your understanding to me.
li-iz-ziz ramanu manahtu-su zid
May my actions be true.
a-mat a-kab-bu-u kima a-kab-bu-u lu-u ma-ag-rat
May the words I speak bring me to success.
is-ti-' nam-ri-ir-ri-ki lim-mi-ru samu kima nasaru sabu-su karabu
May your light shinning in the heavens be a guide to all men you bless favorably.
si-lim itti ya-a-tu-u anaku arad-ka elu
Bless me, a servant of the Highest.
an-un-na-ki ti-i-ru u na-an-za-zu
May the ANUNNAKI come forth and be established.

SATURDAY – SATURN – NINURTA & BA'U

ilu-NINURTA. ilu-NINIB. ilu-istari-BA'U. ilu-ADAR.
NINURTA. NINIB. BA'U. ADAR. SATURN.
siptu aplu gas-ru bukur ilu-ENLIL
Mighty firstborn son of ENLIL.
su-bu-u man-za-za ina ilani rabuti siru rubu-su ilu-ENLIL u ilu-NINMAH
Great is your place among the gods, royal prince of ENLIL and NINMAH.
belu u beltu sihip same u erseti, ilu-NINIB u ilu-istari-BA'U
Lord and Lady of the heavenly abode, NINIB and BA'U,
atwu karabu-ya kisal mahu
Speak favorably of me in your courts,
ana-ku ___ apil ___ sa ilu-su ___ u ilu-istar-su ___
I, ___, son of ___, whose god is ___, and whose goddess is ___.
an-ni pu-tur - sir-ti pu-sur
Absolve me of my sins. Remove my iniquities.
lu-us-tam-mar ilu-ut-ka u atwu ramanu lid-mi-ik
Make me fit to call upon and receive your blessings.
petu babu temu, anaku arad-ka elu
Open the Gates of you Understanding to me, a servant of the Highest,

ilu-istar-BA'U, biltu sur-bu-tu, sela ummu
BA'U, Mighty Lady, merciful mother.
ilu-NINIB, nisirtu qarradu ilu-ENLIL
NINIB, hidden warrior of ENLIL.
ki-bit narbu ramanu zi
Command greatness in my life.
si-lim itti ya-a-tu-u
Look upon me favorably.
sumu-ka ka-lis ina pi nisi ta-a-ab
May your name be in the mouth of the people.
an-un-na-ki ti-i-ru u na-an-za-zu
May the ANUNNAKI return and be established.

SUNDAY – THE SUN – SHAMMASH & AYA

ilu-SHAMMASH. ilu-UTU. ilu-istari-AYA. ilu-SAMAS. samsu.
SHAMMASH. UTU. AYA. SAMAS. SUN.
anqullu u igigallu
Fiery and Powerful One,
dinu ilani
Judge among the gods,
maru aplu ilu-NANNA-SIN
Son of the Moon-god,
sapiru nam-simtu apitu
Overseer of the destinies of the lands.
ilu-SAMAS u ilu-AYA karabu danu simtu
SHAMMASH and AYA, Be the favorable judges of my destiny.
metequ damaqu
May the path be prosperous.
la-kasadu immu kararu
Unequaled light of day,
ilu-SAMAS u ilu-AYA
SHAMMASH and AYA
si-lim itti ya-a-tu-u ___ , apil ___ , sa ilu-sa ___ , ilu-istar-su ___ .
Shine favorably on me, __ , son of __ , whose god is __ and whose goddess is __ .
napahu ramanu sir-tu
Incinerate my iniquities.
lu-ub-lut lu-us-lim-ma maharu nuru
Make me perfect to behold your light.
enu atwu uznu ilu-ENLIL
Lord, who appeals to the ears of ENLIL,

petu babu temu
Open the Gates of your understanding to me.
sumu-ka ka-lis ina pi nisi ta-a-ab
Permanent is your mighty word on earth.
qibitu nig-silim ina ramanu napistu
May your unquestioned command dictate prosperity in my life.
ana-ku arad-ka elu
I am a servant of the Highest,
an-un-na-ki ti-i-ru u na-an-za-zu.
May the ANUNNAKI return and be established.

— D —
: LADDER OF LIGHTS :
INITIATIONS OF ANCIENT MYSTERY SCHOOLS

True esoteric mysteries are often earned by Seekers (and initiates of the *Ancient Mystery School*) progressively through a series of *steps*. The purpose of "grading" is to *gradually* introduce a Seeker to successively "higher" levels of realization and awareness that cumulatively unfold. Various traditions throughout the ages have each interpreted these mysteries differently, adding their own flavors and tables of correspondence, often times obscuring the number of "degrees" to fit their systems: "10 degrees" of the *Golden Dawn*; "33 degrees" of *Freemasonry*, &tc. But, the most ancient famous examples, specifically for our purposes, are described as a "sevenfold" system.

In a conventional esoteric institution, each "level" of initiation—or "step" on the *"Ladder of Lights"*—not only increases a Seeker's awareness of the system, but also grants new potential for personal development. Each *"Key"* is earned while working with a particular fragmented energy "current." These currents have also been called the "seven rays of light" (or the "seven pillars") because they comprise the main tenets of information contained within the structure of form, usually encountered directly in the physical (visible) world of light as "Cosmic Law."

Although the essential existence of the ALL is wholeness, material reality is distinguished by seven bands of a visible spectrum. Each degree appears separate—resonating its own frequency and perceived energy current. Philosophers applied this paradigm to other material spectrums—*seven* notes of music, *seven* colors, *seven* days of the week—each corresponding with one of *seven* physical "celestial spheres" (*planets*), and so forth. The initiate was able to "sample" each aspect of the system in exclusion, and then as incorporated knowledge (with the rest) accumulated as a *"base"* of understanding—a "base" for *awareness* and *knowing*. The Babylonian system of *"Gates,"* levels or degrees, are realized into existence uniquely by different traditions and their practices—all as a result of their *base*. Personal workings are performed from a *"Body of Light"*—the practitioner elevating their consciousness on the astral plane—then intoning specific passwords and names while tracing spiritual gate "seals," "signs" and "forms" that all trigger a preset shift in conscious *awareness* and *knowing*. These "levels" are often associated with "aethyrs" or "etheric planes" of manifestation that is deemed the "Other."

Each level of initiation, step or *"rung"* requires entrance or passage through an *astral gate* equivalent to achievement of further stages of spiritual unfoldment. Similar practices are found in many modern forms of "ceremonial magic," incorporating their own "Ladder of Lights." The Babylonian Star-Gate system—alluded to in all of the Mesopotamian influenced *Necronomicon* cycles of modern esoteric literature—corresponds with an ancient "Mardukite" plan to dedicate and seal the "younger pantheon" of the Anunnaki in Babylon under the reign of *Marduk*. These were to be the patrons of *"New-Babylon,"* a political and spiritual vision that never actually experienced total fruition, but which continues to evolve even today.

The first time Babylon fell, the main priestly class of magicians, priestesses and *Nabu*-scribes moved to Egypt, inspiring an entire "Hermetic" legacy. Modern "Dragon Court" revivals are often led by those with kinship to the Nile Region as well. This does not constitute any genetic propaganda—especially since the dynasties seem to switch back and forth like a pendulum swing, changing with time and politics. Even in Babylon, we see the *"Hand of Marduk"* extend to foreign Kings when necessity demanded. By the time of the "Classical Period," Alexander-The-Great succeeded in taking control of *"dragonblood"* in Egypt, just as he had in Babylon. This over-stretched empire primed weakened conditions on a global scale, eventually leaving the known world wide open to Roman reign, particularly when the Ptolemaic dynasty was "given" to Rome by Cleopatra. Then, when Rome fell, so did its forced "false" authority systems that the world had become dependent on.

The *ankh* was widely known in Egypt as a protective symbol of life—literally the "Key of Life." Few are aware that it also esoterically represented the double-helix serpent-coiled (DNA) and *"Tree of Life"* in Mesopotamia. The *Ancient Mystery School* dedicated the symbol to the AMON-RA in Egypt (also ATEN and "Marduk-RA"). It therefore became highly revered by the Mardukite priesthood altogether. In some traditions, the *ankh* was given (bestowed) to a scribe-priest-magician upon completion of their seventh (final) initiation.

The *ankh* is essentially a "cross," but also and a symbol of "crossings in the heavens"—meaning also "among the stars," or literally "the astral." In one version, the symbol is of the Self standing before the "Omega" shaped gateway. In its original Anunnaki form, this cross is drawn as a "T" (*Tau*) with a serpent being entwined around it. This is where the upper loop comes from, but which continues to coil in an *"infinity-8"* pattern down the stem, simultaneously representing the famous "serpent staff" of ancient magicians.

The serpent is the *"serpent of wisdom"*—*Primordial Dragon*—and equally representing the *"Cosmic Law"* embedded in what humans call "DNA." The Egyptian word: "AN-KH," is very similar to the Sumerian word: "AN-KI," meaning *"universe"*—the ALL—or literally: *"heaven+earth."*

It should come as little surprise that some long-standing esoteric factions of underground society—existing before the modern "Mardukite" inception—made use of these same mysteries: Egyptian Freemasonry and Rosicrucianism. These initiates hold a belief that these "stories of the gods" are in fact literal references to very ancient "luminous beings" (*"Illuminati"*) that eventually *came to be* considered along the same lines as the Olympian Titans. "Tahutian" practitioners—neo-Egyptian dedicates to the embodiment of *Nabu* as the "Thoth-current"—still observe a (self)-initiation system inherited from the Egypto-Babylonian *"Ladder of Lights."* This specific lore has been maintained in an occult manuscript known as the *"Crata Repoa,"* describing seven "levels" of Hermetic initiation.

* * *

A neophyte (first degree initiate) is called the *"Pastophoris."* This is a title bestowed upon the Seeker who has passed the "Earth Gate," and is by nature, a Guardian of the "Gates of Men," and given the secret (pass) word: AMON. They are taught the basic symbolism of the Ladder of Lights and instruction in the physical (natural) sciences. [Mardukite Gatekeepers: NANNA and NINGAL—*"Moon Gate."* Mystical/Temple Craft: Dream Work.]

The second level is called the *"Neocoris."* The Seeker is initiated by "water and serpent" and given physical knowledge of cosmos—the mysteries of geometry, mathematics and architecture. They are bestowed with the "serpent staff," and by the password: EVE, they are granted access to the secret lore of the origins and fall of the human race. Their temple duties include cleaning the pillars (pylons) and generally tending to custodial needs of the shrines. [Mardukite Gatekeepers: NABU and TESHMET—*"Mercury Gate."* Mystical/Temple Craft: Knowledge of Other Minds.]

Ascending to the third step on the Ladder of Lights earn the title of *"Melanephoris,"* when the initiate becomes a Guardian of the "Gates of Death," and perhaps also given the secrets of mummification (a valuable art in Nile Region). Here, the Seeker receives the infamous "Underworld Initiation" after being led to the "Tomb of Osiris" with the passwords: MONACH CARON MINI, meaning: "I count the days of anger." [Mardukite Gatekeepers: ISHTAR and DUMUZI—*"Venus Gate."* Mystical/Temple Craft: Past-Life Memory.]

From this point, the Seeker would be left in the catacombs and archives of lore to discern the secret to access the next level of initiation on their own. If they did not, they would ever remain an initiate of the third degree—but if they were to discover the "secret code," then they would be initiated as a *"Chistophorus"* via the "blindfold rite" (where a red noose is hung around the initiates neck, like a leash). Only then is he allowed to enter the Assembly of the Inner Circle, an Adept among Masters of the Highest Councils. The *"Chistophorus"* is an Adept who has earned the secret of the "shades" (a code for the "primordial battles in heaven" based on the *Enuma Elis*) and given access to the "secret chambers" of the Order. Afterward, the seeker is granted an initiation by fire after proving themselves via dramatically "slaying the dragon" (or removing the head of Medusa/Typhon, etc.) and the password: ZOA. [Mardukite Gatekeepers: SHAMMASH and AYA—*"Sun Gate."* Mystical/Temple Craft: History and Doctrines of the Universe.]

If successful past this point, mystical knowledge comes also in the form of a practical instruction is chemistry and metallurgy as fifth degree *"Balahate"* and the word: KHEMIA or CHEMYA. [Mardukite Gatekeepers: NERGAL and ERESHKIGAL—*"Mars Gate."* Mystical/Temple Craft: Function and Formulas of the Universe.]

After working to master the "godly" understanding of the "heavenly spheres" and the "gods of old," the Adept is the installed to the sixth degree and called the *"Guardian of the Star-Gates,"* or literally, *"Astronomer who stands before the Gate of the Gods"* (a Master-Priest status). Only then are the religious secrets divulged as well as the "true natures" of the Anunnaki, their origins and lore of their rule (and return?) on earth. The seeker is then granted another initiation through the "Gates of Death," this time to meet the Elder pantheon as a true Priest. [Mardukite Gatekeepers: MARDUK and SARPANIT—*"Jupiter Gate."* Mystical/Temple Craft: Material Unity via Love.]

The final and seventh step on the Ladder of Lights is called the *"Saphenath Pancah,"* an initiation required to attain "Prophet" status in the tradition. Secret knowledge of the gods is offered, including privileged knowledge of the "Elixir of Life." The Adept-Master-Priest, now Prophet, is given a white robe [*etangi*] and an ankh to wear. The password of the grade is: ADON (*"Adonai"*), a Semitic name, meaning "Lord of the Earth." [Mardukite Gatekeepers: NINURTA and BA'U—*"Saturn Gate."* Mystical/Temple Craft: Dissolution of Self via Spiritual Unity with the ALL.]

— E —
: ENUMA ELIŠ :
THE BABYLONIAN EPIC OF CREATION

TABLET I

When in the heights the Heavens had not been named,
And the Earth had not yet been named, And the primeval
APSU, who birthed them, And CHAOS, TIAMAT,
The Ancient One, Mother to them all.

Their waters were as One and no field was formed,
No marsh was to be seen;
When of the gods none had been called into being,
And none bore a name, and no destinies were ordained;
Then were created the celestial gods in the midst of heaven,
LAHMU and LAHAMU were called into being
And the Ages increased.

Then ANSAR and KISAR were created,
And the god ANU then came forth who begat NUDIMMUD [ENKI].
Abounding in all wisdom he had no rival.
Thus the Great Gods were established.
But TIAMAT and APSU were still in confusion,
Troubled and in disorder.
APSU was not diminished in might, and TIAMAT roared.
APSU, the begetter of the great gods,
Cried unto MUMMU, his minister,
And said: "MUMMU, thou minister that causes my spirit to rejoice,
Come with me to TIAMAT."
So they went and consulted on a plan with regard to the gods, their sons.

APSU spoke: "Let me destroy their ways, let there be lamentation,
And then let us lie down again in peace."
When TIAMAT heard these words, she raged and cried aloud.
She uttered a curse and unto APSU she asked:
"What then shall we do?"

MUMMU answered giving APSU counsel,

"Come, their way is strong, but you can destroy it;
This day you shall have rest, by night shalt thou lie down in peace."

They banded themselves together
And at the side of TIAMAT they advanced; they were furious;
They devised mischief without resting night and day.
They prepared for battle, fuming and raging;
They joined their forces and made weapons invincible;
She spawned monster-serpents, sharp of tooth, and merciless of fang;
With poison, instead of blood, she filled their bodies.
Fierce monster-vipers she clothed with terror.
With splendor she clothed them, she made them of lofty stature.
Whoever beheld them, terror overcame him,
Their bodies reared up and none could withstand their attack.

She set up vipers and dragons, and the monster LAHAMU.
And hurricanes, and raging hounds, and scorpion-men,
And mighty tempests, and fish-men, and rams;
They bore cruel weapons, without fear of the fight.
Her commands were mighty, none could resist them;
After this fashion she made eleven kinds of monsters.

Among the gods who were her sons,
Inasmuch as he had given her support,
She exalted KINGU; in their midst she raised him to power.
To march before the forces, to lead the host,
To give the battle-signal, to advance to the attack,
To direct the battle, to control the fight,
Unto him she entrusted, saying: "I have uttered thy spell,
In the assembly of the gods I have raised thee to power.
The dominion over all the gods have I entrusted unto him.
Be thou exalted, you are my chosen spouse,
May your name be magnified among all ANUNNAKI."

She gave him the Tablets of Destiny, on his breast she laid them,
Saying: "Thy command shall not be in vain,
And your decrees shall be established."
Now KINGU, thus exalted, having received the power of ANU,
Decreed the fate among the gods his sons,
Saying: "Let the opening of your mouth quench the Fire-god;
He who is exalted in the battle, let him display his might!"

TABLET II

TIAMAT made weighty her handiwork,
Evil she wrought against the gods her children.
To avenge APSU, TIAMAT planned evil,
But how she had collected her forces, the god unto EA [ENKI] divulged.
ENKI was grievously afflicted and he sat in sorrow.

The days went by, and his anger was appeased,
And to the place of ANSAR his father he took his way.
He went and, standing before ANSAR, his father,
All that TIAMAT had plotted he repeated unto him,
Saying "TIAMAT, our mother hath conceived a hatred for us,
With all her force she rages, full of wrath.
All the gods have turned to her,
With those, whom you created, they go to her side.

They have banded together and at the side of TIAMAT
And they advance; they are furious,
They devise mischief without resting night and day.
They prepare for battle, fuming and raging;
They have joined their forces and are making war.
TIAMAT, who formed all things,
And made weapons invincible;

She hath spawned monster-serpents,
Sharp of tooth, and merciless of fang.
With poison, instead of blood, she hath filled their bodies.
Fierce monster-vipers she hath clothed with terror,
With splendor she has armed them;
She has made them tall in stature.
Whoever beholds them is overcome by terror,
Their bodies rear up and none can withstand their attack.

She hath set up vipers, and dragons, and the monster LAHAMU,
And hurricanes and raging hounds, and scorpion-men,
And mighty tempests, and fish-men and rams;
They bear cruel weapons, without fear of the fight.
Her commands are mighty; none can resist them;
After this fashion, huge of stature,
She has made eleven kinds of monsters.
Among the gods who are her sons,

Inasmuch as he has given her support,
She has exalted KINGU;
In their midst she hath raised him to power.

To march before the forces, to lead the host,
To give the battle-signal, to advance to the attack.
To direct the battle, to control the fight,
To him she has uttered your spell;
She hath given to him the Tablets of Destiny,
On his breast she laid hem,
Saying: 'Thy command shall not be in vain,
And the your word shall be established.'
"O my father, let not the word of thy lips be overcome,
Let me go, that I may accomplish all that is in thy heart.
I shall avenge."

TABLET III

ANSAR spoke to his minister:
"O GAGA, thou minister who causes my spirit to rejoice,
Unto LAHMU and LAHAMU I will send thee.
Make ready for a feast, at a banquet let them sit,
Let them eat bread, let them mix wine,
That for MARDUK, the avenger, they may decree the fate.
Go, GAGA, stand before them, And all that I tell thee,
Repeat unto them, and say: 'ANSAR, your son, has sent me,
The purpose of his heart he has made known unto me.

He said that TIAMAT, our mother, has conceived a hatred for us,
With all her force she rages full of wrath.
All the gods have turned to her, with those, whom you created,
They go to her side. I sent ANU, but he could not withstand her;
NUDIMMUD [ENKI] was afraid and turned back.
But MARDUK has set out, the champion of the gods, your son;
To set out against TIAMAT his heart has called him.
He opened his mouth and spake unto me,
Saying: 'If I, your avenger, Conquer TIAMAT and give you life,
Appoint an assembly, make my fate preeminent and proclaim it so.
In UPSUKKINAKU seat yourself joyfully together;
With my word in place I will decree fate.
May whatsoever I do remain unaltered,
May the word of my lips never be changed nor made of no avail.'

Quickly decree for him the fate which you bestow
So that he may go and fight your strong enemy."

GAGA went humbly before LAHMU and LAHAMU, the gods,
His fathers, and he kissed the ground at their feet.
He humbled himself; then he stood up and spake unto them saying:
"ANSAR, your son, has sent me,
The purpose of his heart he hath made known unto me.
He says that TIAMAT, our mother, hath conceived a hatred for us,
With all her force she rages full of wrath."
And he spoke the words of the tale.
LAHMU and LAHAMU heard and cried aloud.
All of the IGIGI wailed bitterly, saying:
"We do not understand the deed of TIAMAT!"

Then did they collect and go,
The great gods, all of them, the ANUNNAKI who decree fate.
They entered in the House of ANSAR, kissed one another,
They made ready for the feast, ate bread,
And they mixed sesame-wine.
They were wholly at ease, their spirit was exalted;
Then for MARDUK, their avenger, they decreed the fate.

TABLET IV

The ANUNNAKI prepared for MARDUK a lordly chamber,
Before his fathers as prince he took his place.
"MARDUK, You are now chief among the great gods,
Thy fate is unequaled, thy word is ANU [ENLIL].
Your words shall be command,
In your power shall it be to exalt and to abase.
None among the gods shall transgress your boundary.
Abundance, shall exist in thy sanctuary shrine,
Even if you lack offerings.
MARDUK, you are our avenger!
We give you sovereignty over the whole world.
Sit down in might; be exalted in thy command.
Your weapon shall never lose its power; it shall crush your enemy.
Lord, spare the life of him that puts his trust in thee,
But as for the god who began the rebellion, empty them of life."

The ANUNNAKI set out a garment

And continued to speak to MARDUK.
"May thy fate, O lord, be supreme among the gods,
To destroy and to create; speak only the word,
And your command shall be fulfilled.
Command now that the garment vanish;
And speak the word again and let the garment reappear!"
Then he spake the words and the garment vanished;
Again he commanded it and the garment reappeared.

When the gods, his fathers, beheld the fulfillment of his word,
They rejoiced, and they did homage unto him,
Saying, "Maerdechai! Maerdechai! MARDUK is king!"
They bestowed upon him the scepter, the throne and the ring,
They give him invincible weaponry to overwhelm the enemy.
"Go, and cut off the life of TIAMAT," they said.
"And let the wind carry her blood into secret places."

MARDUK made ready the bow, his first choice in weapon,
He slung a spear upon him. He raised the club in his right hand.
The bow and the quiver he hung at his side.
He set the FLAMING DISC in front of him
And with the flame he filled his body.
He fashioned a net to enclose the inward parts of TIAMAT,
He stationed the four winds so that nothing of her might escape;
The South wind and the North wind and the East wind
And the West wind He created the evil wind,
And the tempest, and the hurricane,
And the fourfold wind,
And the sevenfold wind, and the cyclone,
And the wind which had no equal;
He sent forth the winds which he had created, seven in total;
To disturb the inward parts of TIAMAT.

Then MARDUK raised the thunderbolt, mounted the chariot,
A storm unequaled for terror, and he harnessed four horses
Named DESTRUCTION, FEROCITY, TERROR,
And SWIFTNESS; and foam came from their mouths
And they were mighty in battle,
Trained to trample underfoot.

With garments cloaked in terror and an overpowering brightness
Crowning his head, MARDUK set out toward the raging TIAMAT.
Then the gods beheld him.

And when the lord drew near,
He gazed upon the inward parts of TIAMAT,
He heard the muttering of KINGU, her spouse.

As MARDUK gazed, KINGU was troubled,
The will of KINGU was destroyed and his motions ceased.
And the gods, his helpers, who marched by his side,
Beheld their leader's fear and their sight was troubled.
But TIAMAT did not turn her neck.
She spit rebellious words.

MARDUK raised the thunderbolt,
His mighty weapon, against TIAMAT,
Who was raging, and he called out:
"You have become great as you have exalted yourself on high,
And your heart has prompted you to call to battle.
You have raised KINGU to be your spouse,
You have chosen Evil and sinned against ANU and his decree.
And against the gods, my fathers,
You have dedicated yourself to a wicked plan.
Let us face off now then in battle!"

When TIAMAT heard these words,
She acted possessed and lost her sense of reason.
She screamed wild, piercing cries,
She trembled and shook to her very foundations.
She recited an incantation, and cast a spell,
And the gods of the battle cried out for their weapons.

Then TIAMAT and MARDUK advanced towards one another,
The battle drew near.

Lord MARDUK spread out his net and caught her,
And the evil wind that gathered behind him he let loose in her
Face when she opened her mouth fully.
The terrible winds filled her belly,
And her courage was taken from her,
And her mouth opened wider.

MARDUK seized the spear and burst her belly,
Severing her inward parts, he pierced her heart.
He overcame her and cut off her life;
He cast down her body and stood upon it.

After slaying TIAMAT, the leader of the ANCIENT ONES,
The might was broken and her minions scattered.
But they were surrounded, so that they could not escape.

MARDUK took them captive and broke their weapons;
In the net they were caught and in the snare they sat down.
And on the eleven monsters which she had filled
With the power of striking terror, he brought them affliction,
Their strength he stole and their opposition
He trampled under his feet.
From KINGU who he had conquered,
He rightly took the Tablets of Destiny
And sealed them with his seal, then hung them from his neck.
Now after MARDUK had conquered and cast down his enemies,
And had fully established ANSAR's triumph over the enemy,
And had attained the purpose of NUDUMMID [EA (ENKI)],
Over the captive gods he strengthened his position,
And he returned to the conquered TIAMAT.
With his merciless club he smashed her skull.
He cut through the channels of her blood,
And he made the North wind steal it away
Outside in secret places between spaces.
His fathers beheld, and rejoiced and were glad;
Presents and gifts they brought unto him.

Then Lord MARDUK rested, gazing upon her dead body
And devised a cunning plan.
He split her up like a flat fish into two halves;
One half of her he established a covering for heaven.
Sealed with a GATE he stationed a WATCHER IAK SAKKAK
And fixed him not to let her waters to ever come forth.

MARDUK passed through and surveyed the regions of Heaven,
And over the Deep he set the dwelling of NUDIMMUD [ENKI].
And after measuring the structure of the Deep,
He founded his Mansion,
Which was created likened to Heaven and he set down
The fixed districts for ANU, ENLIL and ENKI to reign.

TABLET V

MARDUK fixed the Star Gates of the Elder Gods;
And the stars he gave images as the stars of the Zodiac, which he fixed in place.
He ordained the year and into sections he divided it;
For the twelve months he fixed the stars.

He founded his Star Gate of NIBIRU [NEBIRU] to fix them in zones;
That none might rebel or go astray,
He fixed the Star Gate of ENLIL
And IA [ENKI] alongside him.
He opened great gates on both sides,
He made strong gates on the left and on the right
And in the midst thereof he fixed the zenith;
He fixed the Star Gate for the Moon-god
And decreed that he shine forth,
Trusting him with the night and to determine days;
The first of the great gates he assigned to NANNA [SIN]
And every month without ceasing he would be crowned, Saying:
"At the beginning of the month, when you shine down upon the land,
You command the trumpets of the six days of the moon,
And on the seventh day you will divide the crown.
On the fourteenth day you will stand opposite as half-moon.
When the Sun-god of the foundation of heaven calls thee,
On that the final day again you will stand as opposite.
All shall go about the course I fix.
You will drawn near to judge the righteous
And destroy the unrighteous.
That is my decree and the covenant of the first gate."

The gods, his fathers, beheld the net which MARDUK had fashioned,
They beheld his bow and how its work was accomplished.
They praised the work which he had done and then ANU raised up
And kissed the bow before the assembly of the gods.
And thus he named the names of the bow, saying:
"Long-wood shall be one name,
And the second name shall be Dragonslayer,
And its third name shall be the Bow-star,
In heaven shall it remain as a sign to all."

Then ANU and MARDUK fixed a Star Gate for it too,

And after the ANUNNAKI decreed the fates for the ANCIENT ONES,
MARDUK set a throne in heaven for himself at ANU's right hand.

TABLET VI

The ANUNNAKI acclaimed him "First among the ELDER GODS."
MARDUK heard the praises of the gods,
His heart called to him to devised a cunning plan.
He approached IA [ENKI] saying:
"The Key to the GATE shall be ever hidden, except to my offspring.
I will take my blood and with bone I will fashion a Race of Men,
That they may keep watch over the GATE.
And from the blood of KINGU I will create a race of men,
That they will inhabit the Earth in service to the gods
So that our shrines may be built and the temples filled.
But I will alter the ways of the gods, and I will change their paths;
Together shall they be oppressed
And unto evil shall they no longer reign.
I will bind the ELDER GODS to the WATCHTOWERS,
Let them keep watch over the GATE of ABSU,
And the GATE of TIAMAT and the GATE of KINGU.
I bind the WATCHER IAK SAKKAK to the GATE
With the Key known only to my Race.
Let none enter that GATE
Since to invoke DEATH is to utter the final prayer."

The ANUNNAKI rejoiced and set their mansions in UPSUKKINAKU.
When all this had been done, the Elders of the ANUNNAKI
Seated themselves around MARDUK
And in their assembly they exalted him
And named him FIFTY times,
Bestowing upon him the FIFTY powers of the gods.

THE APOCRYPHA OF THE MARDUK TABLET

The Forty-ninth Name is the STAR, that which shines in the heavens.
May he hold the ALPHA and the OMEGA in his hands,
And may all pay homage unto him, saying:
"He who forced his way through the midst of TI.AM.TU without resting,
Let NIBIRU [NEBIRU[be his name—The Seizer of the Crossings
That causes the stars of heaven to uphold their paths.

He comes as a shepherd to the gods who are like sheep.
In the future of mankind at the End of Days,
May this be heard without ceasing; may it hold sway forever!
Since MARDUK created the realm of heaven and fashioned the firm earth,
He is forever the Lord of this World."

ENLIL listened. ENKI heard and rejoiced.
All of the Spirits of Heaven waited.
ENLIL gave to MARDUK his name and title BEL.
ENKI gave to MARDUK his name and title EA and
Said: "The binding of all my decrees, let MARDUK now control.
All of my commands, shall he make known."

The Fiftieth Name is FIFTY and NINNU-AM-GASHDIG,
The Judger of Judges, Determiner of the Laws of the Realm.
By the name FIFTY did the ANUNNAKI then proclaim MARDUK's
 "Fifty Names."
The ANUNNAKI made his path preeminent.

Let the Fifty Names of MARDUK be held in remembrance to all
And let the leaders proclaim them;
Let the wise gather to consider them together,
Let the father repeat them and teach them to his son;
Let them be in the ears of the priest and the shepherd.
Let all men rejoice in MARDUK, the Lord of the gods,

That be may cause the land, his Earth, to be prosperous,
And that he himself may enjoy prosperity!
His word hold and his command is unaltered;
No utterance from his mouth goes unnoticed.
His gaze is of anger and turns his back to none;
No god can withstand his wrath.
And yet, wide is his heart and broad is his compassion;
The sinner and evil-doer in his presence weep for themselves
And pray for forgiveness.

Akhenaton, 32-33
Akkadian, 17, 24, 25-26, 28, 30, 32, 34-37, 43, 50, 52, 57, 70, 87, 101, 107, 118, 125, 135, 141, 147, 158
Amorite, 27-28, 30, 140
Arabian, 18, 24
Assurbanipal/Ashurbanipal, 16, 34, 37, 44, 54, 137, 142
Assur/Ashur, 34, 44, 49, 141, 144
Assyrian, 13, 15-16, 18-19, 24, 30, 33, 34-38, 49, 52, 64, 67-68, 85, 98, 118, 141, 147
Assyriology, 13-16, 37, 147
Borsippa, 35-36, 43, 46, 71, 113, 116
Calah, 19
Canaanite, 18, 25, 28, 121
Chaldean, 20, 27, 34, 36-37, 61, 79-81, 85-87, 89-90, 93, 98, 100, 102, 107, 118, 125, 140
Christianity, 18, 28, 49, 54, 57, 66-67, 73, 75, 86, 98, 100, 103-104, 114, 119, 134
Cuneiform, 15-16, 21, 25, 29, 32-33, 34-36, 39-47, 50, 52, 54, 58, 60, 66-67, 75, 80, 83, 90-91, 102, 106-107, 113, 116, 118, 125, 127, 129, 132-133, 140, 149
Dragons, 31, 46, 52-57, 71, 84-89, 94, 133, 141, 143, 158, 182-184, 186-187, 193
Egypt, 13, 17-19, 21-24, 28, 31, 32-33, 37, 41, 46, 49-51, 53, 58-59, 64, 79, 86-87, 90, 93, 97, 102, 105, 113-114, 118, 120-121, 126, 133, 136, 140-141, 150, 172, 182-183
Enki, 19, 21, 23, 26-27, 29, 40-41, 44-48, 49, 53-56, 58, 61-62, 64, 66-69, 85, 88, 92-93, 97-98, 100, 101-105, 113-116, 120-121, 127, 130, 133, 136, 140-146, 148-149, 160, 163, 172-173, 185, 187-188, 192-195
Enlil, 23, 26-27, 34, 40, 44-45, 49-50, 52-56, 64, 85, 92, 94, 96-100, 101-105, 106-107, 113, 119-121, 133, 136, 140-141, 147-152, 160, 162, 173, 174, 178-179, 189, 192-193, 195
Enuma Elis, 29, 50-51, 53-56, 71, 82, 85-86, 90, 97, 114, 148, 184, 185-195
Erech, 18, 21, 120
Eridu, 18-19, 21, 27, 40-41, 45, 47, 53, 64, 66-68, 101-102, 120, 140
Euphrates, 13, 17, 19, 28, 71
Gilgamesh, 25, 137
Hammurabi, 17, 28, 29-31, 33, 36-37, 56, 129
Hermetic, 49, 51, 58, 64, 69, 75, 93, 97, 113, 143, 182-183
Igigi/Watchers, 40, 53, 64, 94, 128, 132, 147, 189, 192, 194
Inanna/Ishtar, 21, 25, 27, 52-53, 62, 72, 88, 94, 102, 105, 107, 118-124, 125, 127, 132-134, 136-137, 140-141, 159-160, 166, 172-173, 177-178, 183
Islam, 18, 86
Judaism, 18, 28, 49, 54, 57, 66-67, 86, 98, 100, 103, 119

Kabbalah, 50, 58, 61, 63, 67, 69, 89, 105, 119, 142
Kassite, 31, 32-33, 34-35
Khem, 18, 184
Lagash, 16, 18, 27,
Larsa, 18, 125
Lebanon, 18
Magan, 18, 24
Marduk, 19, 23-24, 25-26, 29-31, 32-33, 35, 37-38, 41, 45-48, 49-51, 52-57, 58, 61-62, 64, 66-69, 70-72, 85-88, 92-93, 97, 102, 104-105, 113-117, 119-122, 127, 129-131, 132-137, 140-146, 147-150, 158, 160, 169, 172-173, 176, 182, 188-195
Mari, 28
Mithraism, 18, 49
Nabu, 19, 21, 25, 27, 29, 35-37, 39-43, 44-48, 50-51, 56, 58, 62-63, 65, 66-68, 70-72, 80, 113-116, 120, 127, 136, 141, 143, 149, 160, 165, 172-174, 176, 183
Nanna-Sin, 27, 38, 53, 68, 106-112, 119, 160, 164, 172-173, 174-175, 177, 179, 183, 193
Nergal, 53, 62, 68, 127, 132-137, 149, 160, 168, 172-173, 175, 184
Nile, 17, 19, 182-183
Nimrud, 16, 19, 36, 113
Nineveh, 13, 16
Ninurta/Ninib, 34, 44, 52, 62, 68, 71, 88, 127, 136, 147-150, 160, 170, 172-173, 178, 184
Nippur, 18, 97, 102, 150
Persian Gulf, 18-19, 40, 67, 102
Sargon, 21, 23-24, 25, 27, 29-30, 36, 37
Sarpanit, 46, 50, 54, 62, 64, 72, 113-114, 130, 141-142, 146, 171, 172-173, 176-177, 184
Shammash/Samas, 53, 62, 68, 107, 110, 118, 125-131, 134-137, 160, 167, 172-173, 174, 179, 184
Sippar, 16, 125, 142
Susa, 33
Teshmet/Tasmit, 44, 50, 65, 72, 113-115, 172, 176, 183
Tiamat, 48, 53-56, 81-82, 84-89, 90, 158, 185-194
Tigris, 13, 17, 19, 71
Ubaid, 20, 22
Ur, 18, 20, 27, 28,
Uruk, 17, 18-20, 21, 24, 92
Yezidi/Yazdanism, 18
Ziggurats, 21, 29, 36-37, 46, 50, 58-59, 61, 88, 97-98, 101, 106, 113, 135, 142, 144, 149-150
Zoroastrian, 18, 49, 86, 91

MARDUKITE
10TH ANNIVERSARY

Would you like to know more???

ENTER THE REALM OF THE

**MARDUKITE
CHAMBERLAINS**

**mardukite.com
necrogate.com**

MARDUKITE NEXGEN BOOKS BY JOSHUA FREE

Arcanum : The Great Magical Arcanum : 10th Anniversary —LIBER-A

The Sorcerer's Handbook (of Merlyn Stone) : 20th Anniversary

Necronomicon Anunnaki Bible : 10th Anniversary—LIBER-N,L,G,9+W-M+S

The Sumerian Legacy—LIBER-50+51/52

Necronomicon Revelations—LIBER-R

Gates of the Necronomicon—LIBER-50,51/52+R

Gates of the Necronomicon : 10th Anniversary—LIBER-50,51/52,R+555

Magan Magic (or Necronomicon Spellbook I)—LIBER-E

Maqlu Magic (or Necronomicon Spellbook II)—LIBER-M

Beyond the Ishtar Gate (or Necronomicon Spellbook III)—LIBER-C

Necronomicon Grimoire—LIBER-E,M,C

Enochian Magic & The Kabbalah—LIBER-K

Crossing to the Abyss—LIBER-555

History of the Necronomicon—LIBER-K,555+12

Secrets of Sumerian Language & Cuneiform Dictionary—LIBER-I

Book of Marduk by Nabu—LIBER-W

The Book of Shayaha : Sajaha the Seer of Marduk—LIBER-S

V : The Vampyre's Bible—LIBER-V1

Cybernomicon—LIBER-V2

Vampyre Magick—LIBER-V1+V2

Book of Elven-Faerie—LIBER-D1

Draconomicon—LIBER-D2

Book of Druidry—LIBER-D3

The Druid Compleat—LIBER-D1,D2,D3

The Book of Pheryllt—LIBER-PH1/2/3

Awakening : Systemology-101—LIBER-S1/2/3/4

Reality Engineering—LIBER-S5

Pantheisticon—LIBER-S8

NABU—JOSHUA FREE ("Merlyn Stone")
Chief Scribe & Librarian of New Babylon